FREEDOM FROM FEAR

Taking Back Control of Your Life and Dissolving Depression

By Peyton Quinn

Dedicated to Melissa,
My wife of nearly 30 years

Peyton and Melissa in 1977.

Peyton and Melissa in 2004.

Freedom from Fear:
Taking Back Control of Your Life and Dissolving Depression
By Peyton Quinn

Box 535 Lake George, Colorado 80827
719-748-8555

Second Printing: September, 2004

www.rmcat.com
© 2004 Peyton H. Quinn

ISBN 09759996-0-5

Printed in the United States by Morris Publishing
3212 East Highway 30
Kearney, NE 68847
1-800-650-7888

Table of Contents

Foreward on Depression
by Dr. Bryce Carter

Depression can descend into a person's life at any time and for many different reasons. It often follows a loss, severe disappointment, or serious life set back. Death, divorce, trauma, illness, and job loss are all implicated in the onset of depression. Almost all human beings will experience some or all the symptoms of depression at some point in their lives.

If the depression is of brief duration or the symptoms are not severe, the individual will likely recover with no treatment at all, just as most of us recover from a cold, the flu, and many minor infections without medical care. For a significant number of people, however, the symptoms of depression will last long enough or be severe enough that care will be required. Good psychiatric care can make the difference between suffering from a mild depression and a severe depression, or suffering from a severe depression and suffering from a debilitating, life-threatening depression. Antidepressant medication, talk therapy, and life style changes can all play a major role in alleviating depressive symptoms, returning a person to a state of well being, and protecting against the recurrence of depression.

For individuals attempting to rebuild their lives following depression

One of the most pernicious problems with depression is that the disease and its attendants (lack of confidence, difficulty getting started, a sense of failure, generalized pessimism, feeling inadequate, a sense of being overwhelmed, a sense of lacking control) can insinuate itself into our very identity or sense of self. Past accomplishments no longer supply us with a sense of confidence. Diplomas, awards, and years of service or hard work become pale and insubstantial. Relationships that were once nourishing and vital become burdensome, or we "fake" our way through our interactions and work—unable to live up to our past selves, unable to locate the confidence and ease we once had in our relations and conversations. Activities that we once anticipated with enthusiasm and that we participated in with pleasure lose their allure and become just one more burden in a long string of burdens that ends only with the end of our lives.

If that is all that life is—just a string of moments bereft of meaning, passion, or enjoyment, moments that we must endure or "fake" our way through—then what is the point? Why not end it now? This, for better or worse, is the thinking (often unspoken and sometimes un-thought) underlying depression.

Because depression corrodes our self-confidence, our ability to enjoy relationships, our pleasures in living, and even the very meaning of our lives, the depressed person will often not seek help. What is the point, after all? Depression can also feel more like reality than normal reality does. A depressed reality can feel more real than anything else. At last we know the truth, the depressed person thinks: There is no point to life, it is all meaningless. All that passed before was just an illusion; all our accomplishments were not real, just exercises in vanity and ultimately without meaning. If depression affects the way we think and feel in this manner, it is entirely logical that the individual would not make an effort to seek help. What would be the point when everything is pointless?

Another reason that depressed people do not seek help is to avoid appearing weak. Our society respects self-sufficiency and independence. No one wants to need anyone else's help. Being in need is seen as a kind of failure. So depressed people try to tough it out, try to pull themselves out of it. But this is to underestimate the nature of the enemy. Depression robs us of our strength, motivation. Even our physical energy level drops. Our hope is corroded, our sources of nourishment are stolen, and we are left without resources we need to fight the enemy.

And this is why it is not simply a matter of strength or "pulling yourself up by your bootstraps." There is no strength to be had; there are no "bootstraps" to pull oneself up by.

Unfortunately this is always why the depressed person will often not seek help: out of a desire to avoid appearing weak, or as a manifestation of their loss of hope. That it feels like reality is the nasty aspect of depression. In fact, it can seem even more real than the way life normally seems. "At last I know reality, life is pointless." And, according to some psychologists and philosophers, this realization contains a kernel of truth, that is, that human beings invest life with meaning through love, belief, faith, relationships, creativity, a sense of duty—whatever combination of virtues that allow us to carry on—sometimes joyfully, some times sadly, most times somewhere in-between the two with our life of toil, pain, pleasure, and boredom.

So, how do we turn this ship around, steer it away from the rocky shoals of depression, pointlessness, meaninglessness and toward hope, toward love, toward possibility? Well, if at all possible, the person in the grip of a depression should certainly spend time with a mental health professional to assess the severity and duration of their depressive state and to rule out other possible causes for the symptoms (organic illness, substance abuse, etc.). Once this is addressed, a combination of medication and talk therapy is the recommended treatment for depression.

But what if depression has infiltrated the person's sense of self and chronically impairs their ability to assert themselves, to take on appropriate life and relationship challenges and risks? This is where real life experiences can play a very helpful role. If the person can tackle appropriate life risks—looking for and taking a new job or starting a new business, looking for, beginning, and sustaining relationships, or whatever action would be meaningful and provide the experience of success (however small)—then the path away from failure, lack of confidence, withdrawal has begun.

But what if life in all its randomness and unfairness deals us a set back at this important moment? We all hope that life will be fair and that it will eventually reward our reasonable (and sometimes unreasonable) risks and projects. And those of us who are not depressed recognize this fact, and although we might be disappointed or even partially crushed we are not undone. It is the price one pays for ambition. But for the depressed person, or one not entirely recovered, a set back can be devastating.

Many therapists, myself included, have wished and even tried to provide an opportunity for a person to try out new behaviors to take on safe challenges. If only there was a laboratory for patients where they could challenge themselves to be more assertive, to think more positively, to tackle a situation with confidence with the knowledge that they had nothing to lose. But the dilemma is that if there is nothing to lose, how can it translate into confidence?

The building of self-esteem is integral to the creation of a self that can resist depression. But how is real self-esteem built? It cannot be simply the belief in one's special-ness that some pop psychologists and educators would have us believe. The truth is that we might be special to our loved ones, but in light of the fact that there are simply so many of us, we are not terribly special—we are one of many. And, truth be told, the world would (and will) get along just fine without us.

This does not mean that self-esteem is an illusion; just that self-esteem built on a sense of speicalness or uniqueness is fragile. It is fragile because eventually life will deal us a blow to show us that we are not all that special. Even those among us that have been blessed with unique abilities and great good fortune run into age, disease, death in ourselves and those we hold most dear.

What then can real self-esteem be built upon? The real experiences in life that we are faced with and that we have handled and that we have a real-felt connection with. Now these challenges do not mean that we have to face a tiger in hand-to-claw combat and come out the victor. It simply means we have to face some kind of risk or challenge, try our best, learn from experience, integrate that experience into our sense of self, and take on the next challenge. In this way, bit by bit, challenge by challenge, we begin to see our self as a being capable of handling what life confronts us with, capable of learning from experience, able to experience rejection, setback, and failure without seeing ourselves as failures.

If these experiences and challenges that we face are vital enough, real enough, they do not allow us to fall back into negative thought patterns. They bypass our cognitive thought process and tap into our survival instinct. The famous psychologist Viktor Frankel, who himself survived the Nazi death camps, was reported to have dealt with a suicidal patient by reaching into a desk drawer, pulling out a revolver, and inviting the man to act upon his inclination. A risky move, to be sure, but Frankel was gambling (based on his own intimate experiences with the will to live) that the man's survival instinct would kick in. Sure enough, the story goes, the suicidal man reacted in outrage and accused Frankel of trying to kill him. Deep down below the desire to self destruct, the man's survival instinct was intact and strong. If it is possible for a depressed individual to tap into this survival instinct, it is far stronger than any depression and it will simply force to the sidelines.

But therapy, conducted as it is within the safe confines of the therapy office or hospital, rarely if ever can tap deeply enough into the human psyche to touch upon the survival instinct. Therapy also relies upon language, and the survival instinct is embedded so deeply within our psyches that it predates our acquisition of language. Medication also is only meant to alleviate the symptoms of depression. It cannot reach that deep well of life force that exists within us all.

Now, this is not a call for all depressed people to start parachuting out of airplanes or trying other extreme sports, although under the right conditions that might be an interesting experiment. But under the proper conditions and with experienced coaches and guides, the challenge of facing an adrenaline provoking scenario—custom tailored to the individual's life experience and level of capacity—can be just the thing to tap into that survival instinct that lives deep within all of us.

Now, as a good psychologist I have to say that there has been enough research done on this project to recommend it out of hand. But I am sure that this will strike an intuitive cord with many people, and I encourage you to contact RMCAT or any authorized and reputable organization offering adrenal stress conditioning.

It is my opinion that regularly exercising one's survival instinct innoculates one against depression. the healthy exercise of assertiveness and non-destructive aggession helps to activate our psychological immune system.

Bryce Carter, Ph.D.

Introduction

What are *you* really after in life?

Some of us might say LOVE, others MONEY and still others might be brutally honest with themselves and say POWER.

Yet it isn't really love, money or power that we seek. We seek these things only because we think they will bring us happiness. That is what we are all really after—simply happiness!

We are happy when we are loved and we can give love, when we are physically safe and materially provided for, and when we see a positive future ahead of us.

My late, great father said to me as a child, "Son, you got to have a roof over your head and something in your belly before you can even think like that." Well, as was so often the case, my father was correct, even if as a child I did not understand the extent of his wisdom.

But now, at age 54, I have had my own experiences in life and I have seen that it is also a "spiritual roof" that we need to put over our heads and "spiritual nourishment" that we need to put into our bellies as well.

My personal experiences I speak of include youthful love, abandonment and betrayal, peace and extreme violence, and in my younger days even being the head bouncer in a rough cowboy/biker bar while during the day I was a high school math teacher!

Later I became the three-piece-suited entrepreneur who took an idea and made it into a technology-based company that did very successful business with some of the world's largest corporations. I thus have had the chance to see how various types of people work and think, but most particularly, how predators work and think, be it in the barroom or in the boardroom.

The simple conclusion I reached was that predatory people are fundamentally motivated by the same psychology no matter where you might find them. You may be dealing with some level of predators in the office—perhaps a boss or a middle manager or even a co-worker. You may even have a personal and intimate relationship with an "emotional predator."

Many of us simply do not have the tools or experience to see when we have been chosen as victims by such predators and *why*. Indeed, we may only feel the pain and frustration and internal conflict that the predator causes within us, which may obscure all else.

Countless times I have seen people, often unknowingly, allow themselves to be bullied by one form of human predator or another. Indeed, it is often the "better people," those who are the more empathetic, sensitive and genuinely compassionate, who often seem to attract the predator's eye first.

Yet, being empathetic, compassionate and having a measure of sensitivity to the conditions of others are among the finest of virtues. They are the very source from which the greatest spiritual strength flows. These qualities contain the greatest potential power that a person can possess.

When we cultivate this spiritual strength and learn to use it, we can raise a shield at the predator's first attempt to attack our happiness and our internal self-image. That shield is a mirror of "finely polished steel," and one sees only their own reflection when they look into such a mirror. Hence, the bully sees the face of the bully. He no longer sees a potential victim but only the weakness in his own reflection.

To polish that shield to its full potential, we need to first understand how the bully thinks. We need to understand what he as a bully is really after, and why. The predator's thinking patterns are essentially the same no matter where you find the predator—in the office, in the barroom or in the street.

Once we understand the essence of the predatory mind, we must peel away our own layers of self-deception or "self-misdirection" that we may have constructed to insulate us from a clearer and more authentic view of ourselves. We need to realize that we have been given a "sixth survival sense" that is shared by others in the animal kingdom but from which our socialization often has estranged us. We must allow ourselves to see that while we are far from perfect, we do have an inner strength that lies dormant within most of us. The capacity to actualize that power is given to all of us, but it is only through our own effort that we can *effect the actualization of that inner strength and power*.

There are really only two basic ways to rule a society: through fear or through hope. The same is true of the individual. We can allow ourselves to be ruled by fear, or we can determine that we will rule ourselves through our own positive self-worth combined with rational optimism.

In achieving this we can let go of life goals or "necessary" achievements that are not truly our own but which have been overtly or covertly "assigned" to us by others. You alone must decide your path to happiness, because it is your life and no one else's. This is not an easy task, but then little of value in life is ever achieved easily, is it?

I have not completed the journey down my own path yet, but I do know that my path is the one I have chosen for myself.

In this book I share with you the mental tools, the knowledge and the "weapons of the mind" that I have found effective in the spiritual combat of life. We are all spiritual warriors in a very important sense. Hence, we must learn to think like warriors and to develop the courage of the warrior. The true spirit of the warrior lies not in attacking and plundering the village, but in defending it from those who would.

> *"Know your self and know your enemy and you will be safe in one hundred battles."*
> —Sun Tsu, The Art of War (circa 200 BC)

The Frog Brain and the Self-Image

Living in the 21st century with the body and brain wiring that evolved over thousands of centuries

We are living in a 21st century world with the bodies and "brain wiring" that were developed over hundreds of thousands of years. Since before mankind left the caves, our species has fought a continual battle for survival. Hence, fear and stress have always been part of our environment.

But in our modern world, our evolutionary reactions to stress and fear are less appropriate to the daily problems we now face in our modern lives...either at our jobs or in our personal relationships.

Our biochemistry reacts similarly to the boss chewing us out over a mistake in the office as it did eons ago when we were faced with the danger of taking down a Woolly Mammoth with stone-tipped spears. Our human evolutionary path has left us with some less than truly functional responses to modern life with its new and different forms of conflict.

When we understand this, then we have set upon a path that will change our world view, enhancing and protecting our personal self-images and thus our ability to achieve our goals in this brave new world we live in. In this way we will begin to take back control of our lives.

That, in brief, is the central theme of this book.

In over twenty years of researching and experimenting with human reactions to adrenal stress, it has become clear to me that such stress can re-wire our brain patterns. Recognizing and understanding how this process works can allow us to re-wire our minds and thus our responses, our behaviors and our personal attitudes towards the world and ourselves in a way that makes us more productive and happier. To achieve this requires effort and attention and self-discipline, but I know that it is possible.

To demonstrate how powerful the adrenal reaction is in forming our brain wiring patterns and our resultant behaviors, let me offer what may be a familiar example to you.

The adrenal mind operates at the frog "brain level," not at the self-aware level of our conscious mind.

An example of an adrenal event: teaching your kid to drive.

Imagine that you are a passenger in the front seat of the car and you are teaching your kid to drive for the first time. You are naturally stressed, because for one thing, *you are not in control of the car* anymore. The feeling of not being in control is at the root of a lot of our stressful and irrational fear-based behaviors. Yet, we can't always be in control of everything in our lives. We need to accept this and learn to cope with it.

Now, imagine your kid's driving the car down the street when a second car briskly rolls up to a stop sign perpendicular to your own course. Instantly you stomp at a non-existent brake pedal on the passenger side of the car! In fact, getting no stopping result, you continue to stomp at that empty floorboard repeatedly and furiously!

Why do you stomp your foot? Your self-aware mind knows that there is no brake on that side of the car. But your self-aware mind has been pre-empted by the adrenal memory you have stored from your driving experience. It is the survival brain, the frog brain, that causes your foot to stomp the empty floorboard and *not* your conscious, self-aware mind.

The adrenal memory created by your previous driving experiences (having had to hit the brake immediately in an emergency) conditioned your foot to stomp at a brake when you got the visual cue of an impending collision. Since you were already stressed by not being in control of the car, you were mentally prepped and even over-sensitized to receive that *collision cue*. Consequently, *your body* reacted even when there was actually no real danger of collision. It turned out that the car stopped at the stop sign normally.

Adrenal stress reactions and behaviors become automatic, knee-jerk responses that bypass the fully self-aware mind.

We see from this example how adrenal memories create persistent and automatic responses. These occur at the non-self-aware level of consciousness. Here I have used a physical motor skill as the conditioned behavioral response (stomping the foot on the non-existent brake). But the same thing can apply to our mental processing and to our interpretations of the actions and verbal cues of others.

This is significant, because our response to stress can get pre-consciously programmed into our personal self-images and our personal worldview. In fact, we can automatically respond to something a person says to us in almost the same way as we hit that non-existent brake pedal. We do that without engaging our rational, self-aware minds to evaluate what that person really meant.

Consequently, under stress our personal self-images can change without the intervention of our self-aware conscious minds. The ideal is to prevent this from happening to us and instead to engage our self-aware, rational thought processes when we evaluate and respond to stressful experiences. Your objective is to re-program your thinking so that you can deal with stress-inducing situations in a more rational, more relaxed and healthy way.

Your feelings of positive, personal self-worth must become almost unconditional. Ok, so Judy does not want to go to lunch with you, or you lost your job. You simply cannot let Judy or your job become *the* determinant of your self–image or your self-worth.

Things learned under adrenal stress are stored in the brain differently from non-adrenal events and become more persistent and vivid, pre-conscious memories.

The frog brain is also more directly wired into the olfactory centers and the motor control centers than our self-aware minds are. It was the frog brain that stomped the foot on the non-existent brake pedal. It was not the self-aware mind that caused your foot to stomp, because it knew that there was no brake there. There is often little shared information or communication between these two different brain centers.

Indeed, one of our goals is to establish communication between these two neurological processing centers, the Self-Aware Consciousness and the frog brain. I use the term frog brain because I have been studying this subject and using this term for more than 20 years. But recently neuroscientists use the term Amygdala.

Allow me to give you another example that shows how the frog brain can work. Have you ever rummaged through old things in the attic and then opened a box that released a fragrance that immediately brought back a vivid memory and a flood of emotion? Perhaps it was a memory that you thought you had forgotten. Even a romantic encounter can be an adrenal and other hormonal releasing event.

The frog brain is directly connected to the sense of smell, because smell was critical to finding game food and detecting predators. Detecting the smell of a predator engages the "fight or flight" reaction automatically.

As human beings living in a world of supermarkets and packaged foods, we don't use sense of smell to locate game or detect predators anymore, but the frog brain's special connection to the olfactory center remains the same as it was 300,000 years ago.

The nature of adrenal memories is at the root of understanding Post Traumatic Stress Disorder.

It should not be difficult to see the important role that adrenaline plays in creating Post Traumatic Stress Disorder (PTSD). PTSD is not limited to wartime experience. I have dealt with many people suffering from PTSD who never saw military combat: rape victims, police officers, prison guards, and abused children.

An abusive childhood can be one of the most damaging factors to one's self-worth. But even this can be overcome by understanding the adrenal mechanisms, the true nature of fear, and the way "forgotten" memories can be elicited by environmental cues and cause less-than-rational behavior. Just as the fragrance in the attic automatically brings back a vivid memory, another smell or sound or even humidity can trigger a PTSD episode.

I know of a woman who had been raped by a man who wore large white gloves. Years later she was at Disneyland, and Mickey Mouse approached her wearing large white gloves. She recoiled from the man in the costume. It was only later that her self-aware mind realized why she (that is, her body) had done this.

In another case, a prison guard was conditioned to the sound of running feet as a warning of imminent danger from the prison where he worked. When he was at a shopping mall, he heard the sound of running feet, and his frog brain took over. He braced for combat and scanned everything around him. For an instant he may have even "seen" the prison around him.

Thirty-three years after service in Vietnam, a combat veteran entered a live butterfly exhibit. This was a greenhouse that was kept warm and humid like the jungle where the exotic butterflies came from. High-fidelity speakers played jungle sounds of tropical birds and insects. When the veteran entered the pavilion, he felt nauseous. He collapsed for a few moments and then went outside and quickly recovered. He was not even aware that wartime PTSD had induced the nausea and weakness in the butterfly house.

PTSD is at the extreme end of the spectrum of adrenal trauma or behavioral conditioning. But any event that occurs while we are adrenalized (even if only moderately adrenalized) is recorded and linked to our frog brain. That event may later subconsciously affect our behavior.

An example of an adrenal event in the office

Suppose you are working in an office, and your boss tells you to deliver a report by the end of the day. You are worried, because you realize that it will be impossible to generate the report in such a short time. But you fail to tell him, because your frog brain has been conditioned not to tell the boss that you can't do something.

As the deadline nears and you have not completed the task, you worry even more about the boss's response, and thus you become even less productive. You are flustered and unable to concentrate. In short, your body is in at least a mild adrenal state.

Now imagine that the boss comes into your work area and asks for the report that you have not finished. He gets angry and chews you out, perhaps in front of your co-workers, which greatly increases your adrenal state.

You may feel terrible about the situation and yourself at that moment. You might worry about this after you get home and dread going to work the next morning. In fact, this single incident may color your relationship with the boss and even your job for a long time. But again, why?

The answer is that when we are adrenalized, we are then the most vulnerable to another person re-programming our frog brain level responses to events. In other words, we are creating persistent and vivid adrenal memories of this negative event on the non-self-aware level of our consciousness. The result is that these memories stay with us. But, worst of all we may over time incorporate them into our own personal self-images.

We may start thinking of ourselves as whatever the boss labeled us during the incident. We may begin to see ourselves to some extent as an unprepared or inefficient or even incompetent *person*. At that point the adrenal event has worked its way up into a portion of our self-aware minds and degraded our self-image.

If a parent keeps telling his kid that he is incompetent, the kid will likely grow up believing that he is incompetent, and this can become a self-fulfilling prophecy. As adults, when we are in fear, adreanlized by someone or some event, many of us become like that child again, vulnerable to the actions and belittling words of others.

Do not think this happens only to "wimps" (people who can't take much stress). It has been my experience that the bully is often a coward, constantly afraid of being found out. Yet, from his swaggering and intimidation, you would not call him a "wimp." You might even fear and avoid him. The point is that we are all made of the same clay. While some people handle stress better than others, we all operate under these same basic principles of behavior, especially pre-conscious adrenal conditioning at the frog brain level. We need to be vigilant about preventing this biological chemistry from working against us.

No matter what you call it—cognitive therapy, self-help, or whatever—the real objective comes down to being happier, more at peace, and more productive. When we understand how this adrenal process and our frog brains work, we see how fear controls more of our behavior that we were immediately conscious of.

Our goal is to dissolve irrational fears and to take more control of our lives.

Please understand, I am talking exclusively about irrational fears here, not rational ones. Rational fear serves us; irrational fear does not. Indeed, rational fear can help keep us alive.

For example, when we enter a situation where our gut tells us something is wrong, that there is unseen danger, then something *is wrong*. We should never ignore our gut (frog brain level) feelings. If there is any doubt, then there is no doubt that something is not right!

But irrational fears do not serve us. They can be dysfunctional artifacts generated from our biochemical evolution poorly interfacing and matriculating with our modern social order and its new challenges. Adrenal experiences combined with the words and actions and especially the transgressions of others can cause irrational fears.

In my work at the RMCAT training center, I have encountered many attendants who are highly ranked martial artists. Yet, over the years more than one of them has told me what happened when they went to their ATM machine one night. They saw the homeless guy outside the ATM, and they "sort of knew" that something wasn't right. But they ignored this gut feeling. They ignored their frog brain feeling, and so when the money came out of the ATM, the lights went out for them.

Though full-contact champions in martial arts prize rings, they found themselves helpless to defend themselves against the ambush of a "broken down old alcoholic."

Adrenaline can impair our motor skills, our vision, and our hearing. But most important, it can displace rational thought. This is because most of us are just "not used to it" especially in the context of human aggression. We see the homeless guy outside the ATM, but we are locked into our self-aware conscious mind, so we ignore the very important, visceral frog brain communication of danger. The two neural processing centers are not communicating with each other.

Yet, we have been given the adrenal reaction for its evolutionary survival value, and we can learn to use its power today as well. Understanding and recognizing the adrenal reaction and its physical and mental effects can bring us to actualize its very powerful positive value in stressful situations. This "adrenal advantage" is not limited to physical self-defense either; it enters into every aspect of our lives.

Why are half of all Americans overweight?

To employ a metaphor here, consider that almost half of all Americans are overweight. Now just why is that? Because they eat too much and exercise too little is much too simple and superficial an answer.

Our ability to store fat efficiently had great survival value before modern agriculture and processed food and food preservation were recently developed. I use the word "recently" because compared to the human evolutionary time frame, all of these are very recent indeed.

Consider that up until about 12,000 years ago, our diet consisted almost exclusively of meat and fish, some berries and fruits and was absent of cultivated grains. Our metabolisms and fat storage ability developed when gathering or killing enough food to stay alive was part of our daily fight for survival. Thus, our bodies stored fat reserves for the uncertain times between meals. Our survival depended on efficient fat storage.

But in America today we have an abundant supply of food. Even a good number of homeless people on the streets of

America are overweight. Our fat-storing metabolisms are continually preparing us for a time of starvation that *never comes*. Hence, most of us can build fat easily. Combine this biochemical heritage for fat storage with the type of high-fat fast foods that many of us are "forced" to eat because our "time is pressed," and we have aggravated this fat problem even further.

In a time when food is plentiful, our efficient fat-storing mechanisms are working against our health rather than helping us to survive as they did in the past. Overweight persons are far more likely to develop life-threatening heart disease and diabetes. These burdens of evolution that we have carried into our modern lives are not limited to obesity either. The adrenal reaction leaves us with what are often dysfunctional emotional coping mechanisms when cast against the type of problems that elicit that biochemistry in our modern society. The adrenal reaction was developed to deal primarily with physical challenges, but in today's world most of the daily challenges are psychological and emotional.

Socialization estranges us from a part of our being that we must rediscover.

Of course, that is the very objective of socialization: to estrange us from our socially destructive animalistic and predatory natures. But socialization can have dysfunctional consequences. For example, women have generally been socialized to be much more passive than men. Until recently women rarely engaged in high-contact competitive sports in high school. Yet young men were almost expected to. It was not the intent of this social process to make passive victims out of women. Yet, do you see why the rapist always looks for the more passive, less self-aware woman, the woman with low self-worth and self-confidence? He is not looking for a fight; he is a predator looking for a victim. I have yet to interview a convicted rapist, either in or out of prison, who did not acknowledge that they were looking for a passive victim and not a fight.

This greater passivity often found in women over men is partly a dysfunctional artifact of the socialization process.

However, there is also a clear biological-hormonal component at work here as well. We might speculate that the treatment of women in many societies was an effort to protect women by keeping them more cloistered than young men. But I recognize that some women might argue that point and perhaps rightfully so.

In general, however, our socialization has left most of us, man or woman, ill-prepared to deal with the adrenal stress of direct, stand-up aggression by another human. The human predator today can be found anywhere, and they are not limited to physical assailants. Today they are more often psychological predators.

Most men without military or law enforcement service have seldom, if ever, been in a physical fight. They may not have even faced strong, threatening verbal aggression (except perhaps on that long-ago middle school playground). A great many of us are estranged from our survival instincts through imperfect socialization. We are left impaired in dealing with even just "right in our face" verbal abuse.

The true predator, some of whom are in prison and a good number of whom are not, recognize this. They even count on it. They are bullies, because they have learned that most people will just "choke up" or hesitate under aggressive posturing and verbal threats.

Again, the bully in the office may not try to rape you or beat you up, but he or she works on the fundamental assumption that most of us are socialized out of effective resistance and can be ruled by fear. The bully knows that if they can make you afraid, they can control you. If the bully can even moderately adrenalize you, then he or she knows that they have gained some control over your mind. We have been socialized such that we are often ill prepared to deal with the human predator, whether in the street or in the office.

From my experience and observation, I submit that human predators exist on a very long continuum. Indeed, though it is repressed, it is somewhat ironic that all of us still have at least some small part of the predator remaining in us too, even if it is deep down inside. Socialization has thus estranged us from an important part of ourselves.

We all have survival instinct. When that is engaged, our predatory instincts come into play. In an extreme case where you must protect your family, the tactical situation may compel you to set up an ambush for the "prey" as they seek your family. These people are threatening your family. You become the "hunter predator" by setting up the ambush for them even though you are acting in response to their aggression.

You would be surprised what people have inside when it comes to protecting their families and children. It is even more powerful, devious, and tactically well-executed than if they alone were in danger. By pondering this reality, the reader is planted with the seed that he or she can actualize the predator within him or herself if the situation demands that.

On a much less stressful level, just saying to someone "I told you so" reflects the shallowest level of our predatory instinct.

Nature will not be denied. It will express itself one way or another. If we can experience and recognize, strengthen and control key portions of that part of our being that our social order and upbringing have separated us from, then we become more complete, competent and self-actualized. We can then deal with the bully or the pressures of the office or other job scenes more out of our own rational self-awareness than by intermittent, irrational, fear-based thinking. That irrational thinking results, in part, from our separation from that inner, more primitive "self."

That is the real basis of our fear too. Having been estranged from our survival self through socialization, we often don't know what to do when faced with the predator. It is somewhat like a deer caught in the headlights of an oncoming car. The deer has only developed two evolutionary responses to danger: Stand still and hope the predator does not see them, or run!

But the oncoming headlights are a new variable that was not present during those eons of evolutionary development. Hence, the deer does not know what to do, either. It may freeze in the headlights and get struck by the car.

We can freeze up, too, in the face of aggression and danger just as the deer did. But, as human beings we have a higher central nervous system than that deer, and we can reason our way to new options. But that reasoning is best and most effective when we do it *before* we become the target in those "headlights."

Getting in touch with our frog brain's communications does not mean that we become more animalistic. It is much more like we become the experienced horse race jockey. We ride on top of that powerful race horse within ourselves, guiding and pacing that beast to cross the finish line first. We can learn to control that beast within us all; so it does not control us.

When we accept and recognize and then discipline that part of ourselves that socialization has partially subjugated, we become more complete and rational. We become spiritually stronger. All compassion comes only from spiritual strength and wholeness, just as all cruelty comes from weakness and fear.

My first "laboratory" for the observation of the ways of human predation and the adrenal stress reaction: a biker bar

Many years ago (after the Earth cooled and the dinosaurs came), I was a mathematics teacher in a New Mexico high school. The job barely paid enough for me to live on. After an incident in the only bar in town (and a very large and rowdy bar it was, to say the least), I was offered a job as a bouncer on weekend nights.

I was naïve about the job. But that rather curious employment gave me a tremendous opportunity to observe the mechanics and psychology of human aggression and predation. The bar was like a living laboratory to me. Later in life I discovered that the lessons I had learned in that bar applied to the corporate boardroom as well. It was universal knowledge about how the human mind and brain work, especially under adrenal stress.

There can be plenty of stress in a boardroom or in high-stakes contract negotiations with a giant corporation too.

I have set my feet in both these worlds, and I came to see that most counter-productive behavior and most irrational decisions people made in any of these environments were chiefly the result of fear.

Yet the people making these decisions or behaving irrationally seldom saw this. This was because their response to fear had mostly been formed by their autonomic frog brain wiring: the same part of the brain that reflexively and less than super consciously stomped at that non-existent brake pedal on the passenger side of the car.

One of the most important things I learned as a bouncer trying to maintain order in that madhouse of a bar was how to deal with hostile and aggressive people. This was made possible partly by coming to understand the true motivations and ways of the human predator and seeing the fear-based element in their behavior... and learning to control mine.

At first it is not easy to see that a guy towering over you and threatening to bust your head open, festooned with demonic tattoos on his gigantic arms, is driven by fear. This is because he is *scaring the living hell out of you!*

But here is the key: That is precisely why he is threatening you. He wants to elicit your fear, and that is also why he has those tattoos. It is why he is dressed as he is. Fear is also why he has worked out with weights.

The bully is often the coward constantly afraid of being found out. Even so, if you do not handle him right, he might well stomp your head in. Keep in mind that we are all made of the same clay and that bullies of all stripes are found in barrooms and boardrooms and many other places. The office bully fundamentally works the same way "brain wiring wise" as the barroom bully. It's just that the consequences and their methods differ.

If you do not handle the office bully correctly, then instead of getting your head stomped in you might get fired or never get promoted. The office bully can soak up so much of your life's energy that your work environment can become hellish to you and difficult to let go of when you get home.

These are some of the problems we are going to address in this book as well as strategies to overcome or escape these negative life-impacting situations.

Understand how predators and bullies think.

The first key is to *understand the predatory mind* so we can use logic to deal with the predator and bully, no matter where or on what level of society we may encounter them.

When I first starting working in that bar, I did not realize these things. Consequently, I got into a lot of fights with the barroom bullies. At first this happened almost every weekend, because I did not know how to handle these guys to avoid violence. My responses to these cretins were mostly from my frog brain and thus fear-based at that early stage of my bouncer career.

But necessity is the mother of invention, so I found new ways to handle them other than with the edge of my hand or a hard-driving elbow. These new ways were based on seeing what motivated them and then playing off their own brain wiring.

Because I came to understand the ways of the predator, I was able to avoid two-thirds or more of the fights that I had previously gotten into. Yet the only thing that changed was my behavior toward potential assailants. I learned to manage my fear and to listen to my frog brain's signals without being overcome by them.

The following incident occurred during my bouncer work. It underscores some of these principles as they applied to dealing with three semi-adolescent predators. Understanding these same human behavioral models later served me well in both sales and business management.

Date: September 1975

The Place: A large and rowdy New Mexico bar

My Job: To stop or at least contain violence as head bouncer

When I saw the three young men come through the door, I knew immediately that they had come to prove to themselves that they were "real men." They needed to quiet their secret fears that the other bar patrons might see them as potential victims rather than "real men." To fill this need and to over-come this fear, they would start a fight. It could be over any-thing: an insult or any show of disrespect to them, real or imagined. It just did not matter.

I felt that I was watching a human version of Mutual of Omaha's television series *Wild Kingdom*. Fortunately, by that time in my "career" I knew the ways of these neophyte preda-tors. I knew the real reason they had come into my bar. It was not really a fight they wanted. That was only a means to their end. Their real objective was overcoming their fear that they might be seen as less than "real men" in this modern jungle of tough guys. I also knew that there were plenty of real tough guys in there quite willing to fight these guys at the slightest op-portunity.

My job was to prevent violence. I would accomplish this by giving these three men what they had come in for in the first place. There would be no fighting. Further, they would be happy about that, too. And they would feel better about it than if they had kicked everybody's ass in that whole bar of 500-odd people.

As soon as the trio sat down at a table, I pulled up a chair, uninvited of course, and plopped myself down with a show of fatigue.

"Look at this place, dudes," I said. "There must be 500 peo-ple here tonight, and my job is to keep order? And with just six other guys to help me? Look, the instant I saw you guys come through that door, I knew you dudes had been around a bit and could take care of yourselves. I'll bet you guys can spot a fight before it even starts. Am I right?"

They acknowledged that they had been around and could take care of themselves.

"Dudes, I'm asking you for a little help here. I can't be ev-erywhere at once, and I sure don't want you to get physical with anybody, but I know you've got the experience to spot trouble before it even gets physical. So if you see a fight brewing in this part of the place, would you guys just give me the high sign so I can cool it down before it gets physical?"

They agreed to do so, and I knew right then that it was un-likely that I'd have any problem with them. In fact, in time they became semi-regulars and they took their "stations" each time they came in to give me the "high sign" if they spotted any po-tential trouble.

What three young men needed and what they really feared.

These young men were afraid that if they did not appear to be tough, they would be seen as victims. They were afraid some real tough guys might either beat them up or verbally humiliate them in that bar. That is what they truly feared.

They didn't really want a fight but rather a show of respect. To achieve that, they were willing to start a fight to show that they were not easy victims. This was, of course, fear-based irra-tional behavior. When I asked for their help, they got their re-spect. Hence, they did not need to fight.

Further, I knew that my talking with them would not go un-noticed by the other more experienced predators in that bar. That would discourage the other tough guys from seeing these three young men as suitable "safe victims" too.

The most dangerous predators

I am now going to offer an extreme case of the same fear-based brain wiring in action, only in the much more deadly environment of a maximum security state prison.

Prison is a crucible and a cauldron of some the most danger-ous predators. That is precisely why many of them are there, of course. Prisons provide us with a focused and illuminated view of how the irrational, fear-driven mind of a violent criminal predator works. If we can understand why a convict would kill another man over a single cigarette, then we begin to under-stand the human predatory mind at its worst.

If we can come to understand the act of killing over a ciga-rette, then it should be much easier for us to understand a sales prospect's objections, or the way we need to approach upper management to achieve professional goals, or how we should treat a subordinate employee to earn his trust and support. All these things exist on the same long continuum and share important behavioral elements.

Why would a convict feel he had to kill another inmate over a cigarette?

I have interviewed a number of convicted killers, drug dealers and armed robbers in researching the predatory mind. I have used this research to help develop my self-defense and self-improvement training programs at the RMCAT Center on my ranch in Colorado.

Some of the crimes these convicts commit are difficult for the healthy, rational mind to even grasp. Senseless killings are almost common in some prisons. Prisons can be bloody, boiling cauldrons of the most dangerous human predators. This particular homicidal drama, in brief, goes like this:

One convict bums a cigarette off another. The convict is expected to repay the cigarette later. However, he fails to repay the cigarette, and the first convict retaliates by coming up behind him, stabbing him repeatedly with a make-shift "prison shank," and killing him.

The normal mind asks, "Why kill over a cigarette?"

Though not easy to see at first, the answer is in the same pattern of fear-based behavior of the three neophyte predators who came into my bar looking for a fight. The convict did not really kill the man over the cigarette. He killed him because in not paying back the cigarette, *the second convict showed disrespect.* He was not giving what convicts refer to as "props," meaning "proper respect."

The convict sees "props" as essential to survival, because without them, he becomes identified as a potential victim in an environment of the most vicious predators. The slightest show of disrespect in prison can demand the most drastic, lethal retaliation.

This is just a more extreme example of the irrational behavior of the three young guys who came into my bar afraid that they might be seen as potential victims. The convict who killed over a single, un-repaid cigarette was afraid that if he did not, the other convicts would see him as a "safe victim," leading to rape or death. In both cases we have a similar pattern.

The patterns of thinking of predators and bullies is similar in whatever environment they might be found.

From the young men in my bar trying to act tough to avoid being seen as easy victims, to the homicidal prison convict who killed over not getting his "props," we observe the same fear-based irrational behavior. But it is often much more difficult to see that behavior in ourselves.

Let's return to our office worker given the task of generating the report by the end of the day. The employee knew the deadline was hopeless. But out of fear, he said nothing to the boss. It was irrational, fear-based behavior not to tell the boss that the deadline was unreasonable. This behavior had most likely been conditioned into the employee by previous stressful episodes with the boss.

In not communicating with the boss, the employee was programming himself for even greater failure. If the employee had a stronger, less fearful, less externally qualified self-image, he might have handled the situation more rationally. That would mean programming himself for success rather than failure. Let's see how that dialogue might play out:

Having a non-reactive, non-fearful mind in the office setting

Suppose your boss says to you, "I want this report by the end of the day." That is the time to negotiate whether this expectation is reasonable or even possible.

You might say: "Mr. Smith, to do that I will have to draw all the records from 2002 and 2003 and flag those specific accounts that you need to quantify. Our software is not set up to do that, so a lot of this will have be done manually. That will take more time than remains in this day. But I feel confident that working hard at it, we can have it done by about 2:00 p.m. tomorrow."

Here we are concentrating on what we *can* do rather than what we can't do. What we can do is get it done by 2:00 p.m. tomorrow. But if you allowed your fear of Mr. Smith to overcome your realistic judgment, then you would not say the above, would you? You would act out of the re-active, fear-based mindset and would allow your re-active mind to set you up with an unrealizable goal.

Further, by not speaking up at his unreasonable demand, you would be enabling Mr. Smith's over-demanding behavior. That behavior would continue and even escalate later.

Fear drains much more of our life's energy, or essence, than does hope or acceptance of the reality of a situation. We must first protect ourselves. That means speaking up to authority and never tolerating abuse from anyone.

The ability to do this depends on self-acceptance and a positive self-image. When we accept ourselves, we accept our strengths and our intrinsic value as a unique human being. Having accomplished this, then we can logically and pragmatically analyze our limitations.

Sometimes those limitations are self-imposed by irrational fear. Other times they are simply the reality of the situation. But fear can prevent us from distinguishing between these two types of limitations.

Again I will return to my experience as a bouncer to underscore common attributes of predators and bullies, whether in the bar or in the office. Understanding the predator is essential to recognizing them and protecting ourselves from them.

How predators choose their victims

The predator realizes that he or she may become the victim themselves if they choose the wrong person to abuse. The extreme criminal predators are the ones most keenly aware of this. This is because they became predators from watching "role models" who abused them. This could be an absentee or abusive father, mother, a sibling, or the other kids and bullies in the street.

Consequently, the predator will almost always *test* their chosen victim for "safe victim potential" before abusing them. This is true no matter where on the continuum the predator lies. That continuum ranges from our convict "cigarette killer" to the verbally abusive or exploitive office co-worker or over-bearing manager.

Many years ago my bar/bouncer work showed me the predator's repetitive habits. As I mentioned previously, later I saw similar patterns in the corporate world and elsewhere. The difference was just a matter of degree and of consequences, really. But in all walks of life you are going to encounter some type of predator searching for victims. We had best learn how they operate and thus how to deal with them.

An example of the barroom predator's "interview" modus operandi

Several times as a bouncer I would see a tough guy at the bar scanning others to decide who could most safely be verbally abused. He would then look at the selected victim and say something like, "What the fuck are you looking at dickhead?" or something equally original, eloquent and poetic.

The passive response

Now, if the victim of this verbal challenge ignored it or denied what was happening, the predator would be encouraged to go to phase two of his "interview." This is because the predator would see fear in his victim's denial.

The bully's objective is to instill fear in his victim to paralyze their thinking and/or their ability to defend themselves. He wants to see some expression of fear before he proceeds.

Seeing denial, the barroom predator would then amplify the insult or threat to further test the victim before he went all the way. "All the way" might mean coming over to the guy and punching him out, or perhaps thoroughly humiliating him verbally until he left the bar. The bully gets temporary relief from his or her own deep feelings of inadequacy and powerlessness by abusing others with impunity.

The aggressive response

If the intended victim did not ignore the predator but gave him an aggressive reply such as, "I think I'm looking at two pounds of shit in a one pound bag," then he would have escalated the situation and given the predator *no honorable way out.* The predator would either have to back down or go ballistic and attack. This escalation strategy is not the best one. The bully has been given no honorable exit.

The predators in the office or on the street or in the barroom all operate in fundamentally the same way. Consequently, this aggressive escalation strategy often fails in any of these arenas. But as we have seen, the "ignore him and he will go away" strategy that we may have been taught as children isn't the best one either. The hard-core predator will even see your being "reasonable" as weakness. This type of predator often sees human compassion as the ultimate weakness.

The predator's interview—whether in the office, the bar or the street—is an intelligence-gathering mission to see if you are safe to abuse.

Understanding and recognizing the bully's "interview"

You will find people at every point on the predatory continuum engaging you in an "interview" to determine your suitability for exploitation. The best time to establish that you are not a suitable victim is at the interview. You never get a second chance to make a first impression.

In our previous office scenario, the employee should have told the boss upon being given the impossible deadline that it could not be completed until 2:00 p.m. the next day. Failing to say that greatly aggravated the employee's fear, frustration and loss of self-worth.

If you are the guy at the bar chosen by the barroom bully as a potential victim, recognize at once when he is starting his "woof" (interview) and shut it down at the very beginning. Actually, if you study this book, internalize the lessons and breathe them into your soul, it is unlikely that the barroom bully will choose you for his victim anyway. He will already see that you are not a victim.

Dealing with the predator's interview

There are not too many hard and fast rules in life, but the following come pretty close to it. I will point out that I discovered these rules the hard way. Every decent prison guard or effective salesperson or State Department ambassador knows these truths about dealing with potentially hostile people too.

1) Do not insult them.

2) Do not challenge them.

3) Give them as easy and as honorable a face-saving exit as you can.

4) Show no fear. (This may not always be the same as feeling no fear.)

The difference between being assertive and being either aggressive or passive

Observe that insulting the predator during the barroom interview will escalate the situation and break at least the first three of the four rules in dealing rationally with predators. In fact, some predators are experienced enough to see that a show of bravado is fear-based as well. Thus, the potential victim has broken the fourth rule too.

The person who escalates the predator's interview by hurling back his own insult might back the predator down. But at some point his escalation of the conflict may force a fight. That "fight" may be physical as in the barroom or political as in the boardroom.

In an office setting, an aggressive response may just get a person fired if the predator is an insecure middle-level manager who is yelling at an employee. An aggressive response can occur even though the employee is consciously aware of the potential negative consequences. This is because the employee's irrational brain wiring kicks in and responds for him. This type of aggressive behavior seldom serves us in this context. Fear-based frog brain emotions are born from the reactive mind.

Hence, we must train ourselves to avoid unconsciously surrendering our psyche to that irrational semi-self-aware brain wiring that is mixed in with a portion of our frog brain. Understanding the modus operandi of predators can help us greatly in that effort.

The passive individual who ignores or denies the threat spells "lunch is served" to the predator. Never let yourself be placed in a subservient role by the other party in any negotiation. Make no mistake about it: When you are insulted or challenged like this, be it in a barroom or in the office, you are being "interviewed" for victim potential, and so the "negotiation" has begun. This can be a "negotiation" with an aggressive panhandler or even a sexist remark by an office co-worker. It is important that you recognize the first signs of the interview and know when a predator's game is afoot. You must know immediately when you are being interviewed and why.

So what do you do? Being aggressive is dangerous and often fails. Being passive is an invitation to being abused. The answer is to *be assertive.*

Being assertive

When we are assertive we set a boundary—often just a simple, clear, firm verbal boundary.

A good example of being assertive in the office comes from an attendant in one of our RMCAT classes who emailed me some time ago. She told me that Mr. Brown had for two years habitually made off-color and unwanted sexual remarks to her and in the office.

She had previously ignored him, so his offensive behavior continued and even escalated. When she took our scenario-based course, she knew intellectually and also experienced *viscerally* why ignoring the predator was not the correct strategy.

After she took the course and got back to the office, before she had even fully realized it, she jumped to her feet when he made his first remark, and she shouted, "Mr. Brown, I will absolutely not tolerate this type of behavior from you one minute longer!"

Mr. Brown's eyes got big, his face flushed, and he took two steps back at the ferocity of her verbal boundary setting. Every eye in the office was on him. Mr. Brown left the room and never bothered her again. Some weeks later he came to her and apologized for his previous behavior. He said that he had not realized it had upset her so much. This, of course, was not the full truth, but predators can sometimes fool even themselves.

She told me that she was proud of herself for doing this. But she was also a little upset with herself too for allowing it to go on for two years when this was all she had to do to stop it. All she had to do was to establish a ferocious verbal boundary and to refuse the victim status that he had imposed on her.

Her previous passivity had allowed Mr. Brown to place her in a subservient negotiating position. She had missed her opportunity to set that boundary at Mr. Brown's initial "interview" (that is, the very first time he made a sexual remark). The initial interview is always the best time to shut down any type of predator. Fortunately, her later forceful verbal boundary succeeded in changing that relationship entirely.

Let's shift gears a bit now and see how this same concept was applied to the corporate world. I will begin with a little background so that you can better appreciate my situation at that time.

Date: 1986

The Place: A giant glass tower office building in Denver, Colorado

My Job: Secure the first software development contracts ever outsourced for ATE work for IBM

My goal was to start a company. I had spent nearly a year on my own (without pay) trying to raise $350,000 to start a specialized software development company. My bank account was just about dead empty. I also had a mortgage, insurance, car payments, and other monthly bills.

Hewlett Packard had released a new series of Automatic Test Equipment (ATE) that performed electronic tests on circuit boards before they were installed in the finished product. However, these new test machines had to be specifically programmed for each different circuit board. This programming demanded fluent knowledge of the newer version of HPL (Hewlett Packard Programming Language) as well as the capabilities of this new ATE device.

The entrepreneurial opportunity I saw lay in the fact that almost no one possessed that level of knowledge and experience besides the technicians at HP itself. I also knew that those HP technicians were non-college-degree engineers.

Their lack of a college degree in electrical engineering capped their income potential within HP. I knew that some of them were not happy with the way HP management treated them. They occasionally assigned them to tasks that the engineers felt were beneath their talents and special skills. (These technicians felt that they were being denied their "props.")

HP had a policy of not getting directly involved in programming their ATE equipment. Yet IBM had significantly underestimated the time it would take them to get their engineering programming staff up to speed on this new version of the HPL language and the ATE machine. That time lag could cost IBM several million dollars.

My plan was simple: I would get conditional and confidential employment contracts with the technicians at HP to work for my new firm if and when I raised $350,000 to start the company. This was a "chicken and egg" challenge. I could not get the money until I showed I could get the contracts from IBM. But how could I get the IBM contracts without the money to actualize the employment contracts with the HP technicians and also to buy the new ATE programming stations to develop and test the programs?

I used my Amex card (not having any idea how I would pay the bill when it came in if my plan failed) to fly down to an IBM manufacturing plant and discuss things with their engineering group. It was clear to me (though they tried not to display it directly, of course) that these IBM people knew that they were in some real career trouble if they could not get the new ATE equipment programmed and on line shortly after it was installed.

All the signs of fear were there. Among other things, a few senior-level people in the engineering group were asking to be transferred to other departments. This, I concluded, was so that they could distance themselves from any failure that they saw coming in programming the new machines. "Know your enemy and know yourself and you will be safe in 100 battles," Sun Tzu, The Art of War, circa 200 B.C.

You must recognize fear-based behavior in any negotiation. But it is generally not strategically correct during the negotiations to acknowledge that you see that fear in your opponent. This denies them their "props" and tends to polarize things. (However, you must always recognize and acknowledge your own fear-based behavior to yourself.)

Some weeks after that visit with the engineers at the IBM plant, I was in a large office in a giant glass tower in Denver. I was waiting for two members of IBM's accounting and one senior management person to enter.

I examined the logistics of the "battlefield." I was sitting at the end of a long, polished walnut table in a comfortable office chair. At the opposite end of the table were three larger empty chairs. One chair was directly opposite mine at the other end of the table. The other two chairs flanked each side.

Whoever sat in the chair directly opposite mine was going to be the real decision maker. I assumed that would be the senior-level manager. An experienced commander will sometimes allow their first officers to attack while he watches for weakness in his opponent. I anticipated and prepared for this.

As the IBM crew entered, they seemed not just in good humor, but in a light and very casual state of mind. It was as if they were non-verbally projecting the idea that nothing really important was going on *for them* at that meeting. This was not the serious attitude that I had anticipated from them in these negotiations. We shook hands, smiled and exchanged the normal courtesies before they took their chairs. I could not hear what one said to the other as they walked to the end of the table. I do not think I was meant to, either.

The majority of human communications is non-verbal. There is a great deal to be inferred from facial expressions, the walk, the eyes, the movement of hands, etc. Their walk was not a swagger, but I got their unspoken message before their corporate butts even hit the leather of those office chairs. Their attitude was, "We are Big Blue, so we don't really need you of course, but we are granting you the courtesy of a hearing today."

I could not allow the negotiations to start off on this note. I would fail if I allowed my opponent to place me in an initial subordinate negotiating position. To prevent this I had to act preemptively.

It was similar to when I really knew a guy was about to throw a punch at me in my bar work. I would not wait for his shot to come. I would act first. Here, I had to speak first. I think the IBM guys did not expect that either.

"Mr. Harding," I said, "I am very happy and excited to be here today because I see very clearly that we have the precise elements necessary to make a mutually profitable business relationship. Your engineering department has correctly identified a significant potential problem, and today we are taking positive action to solve it before it becomes a really big problem.

"My staff will solve your problem by greatly accelerating your engineering team's success with this new equipment. My estimation is that given the quality of people that I met with in your manufacturing plant, that perhaps in as early as six to eight months from now they will be as experienced as my team in applying these new systems. But in the meantime, we can make sure that you have the new programs running and that your production line is pumping out a thoroughly tested and quality product. Isn't that what we both want, sir?"

Now, what could Mr. Harding say to this? Could he say, "Not hardly kid, we can handle our own ATE programming needs just fine"? This would be the "I don't have a problem that needs your solution" type objection. Or perhaps he might say, "Oh, it really isn't so important to get this stuff on line so fast. We've gotten by this long without any outside help." This would be the "There is no hurry to get your solution in place, we have gotten by fine this long without it, no hurry to make a decision now" type of objection to the sale.

No, if he took any of those positions, we would not have gotten into that negotiation room in the first place. What Mr. Harding had to find out was could we do it, and how much did they need our solution if we could?

I had come well prepared to demonstrate and document that my people had done this type of ATE work for sometime and to the highest standards. Showing them that they needed our solution had to be handled sensitively so they wouldn't perceive this as a challenge to their own people's competence. That would mean disaster for me, as I might then be seen as challenging the foundation of their self-images—that is, as the "big boys from Big Blue."

Of course "my staff" still worked for HP and not for me yet, and that was a tricky situation. But I structured things so this never became an issue or was even apparent or addressed during that meeting. I did, after all, already have an employment agreement with the technicians at HP.

I got the contracts from IBM, then the $350,000 to activate the employment contracts. This was completed in less than two weeks from the limited partners we had already assembled.

But what if I had worried too much about how I would pay my American Express bill if I failed? In that case I would never have started, because I would have not flown down to IBM to meet with their engineering group. I would never have started the ATE company. Risk is life, life is risk. We have to define our goals and prepare for the accompanying risks and not allow our fear of failure to chain us to our "desks."

Now you might say, "OK Quinn, you did a good sales job on the three guys who came into the bar for a fight and on the IBM people too. But so what?"

In an important sense, we are all in the business of sales.

No matter what our profession, we are all selling. We are all salesmen or saleswomen by default. A doctor sells medical services. He also tries to sell his patient on following his medical program. A lawyer sells legal services. He tries to sell his view of a case to a jury, and he sells his clients on taking his legal advice. A car salesman sells cars, and a politician sells himself and sometimes his ideas. A laborer sells his labor. A suitor tries to sell his worthiness to a woman he wants to marry, or a playboy may do the same for a girl he wants to bed.

But, it is all sales in the largest sense, isn't it? It may help to accept that sales itself is an honorable profession *if conducted honorably*. Can you really sell something to someone that they do not want or need? Can you really profit by cheating on a sale? That is, taking more or delivering less than was promised or by using deception? I have met a good number of people over the years who thought so, but not one of them that I know of succeeded on a long-term basis. They all ultimately failed.

Sales is the art of communicating and dealing successfully with people. Isn't that a major part of the "art" of "living successfully" itself?

What is self-defense?

Self-Defense is the art of dealing with predators—exploitive, hostile or abusive people. As we have seen, they can be found in any sphere of our lives: in the street, at the office, at home, and even in intimate relationships. Consequently, when I use the term "self-defense" I am not *just* talking about defending yourself against the person who wants to beat you up, kill, rob, or rape you.

Even so, do not dismiss the reality that you may be forced to deal with physical violence. Prepare for that terrible possibility. These terrible things don't happen only to others. Self-defense is anticipating possible threats and situations that you might find yourself in and then developing a reasoned and practiced plan to deal with them.

Yet most likely you will have to deal with just an unpleasant or verbally or psychologically abusive person rather than the outright violent criminal assailant. We can thus see the idea of "self-defense" in this much larger context just as we might see the concept of "sales" in its greater context.

Self-defense is a subset of the larger goal of self-improvement.

Self-improvement and self-defense both involve preparing yourself for success before you enter the arena, in whatever form or place that arena may be. Of course there is much in this world that is simply beyond our control. We have to recognize and accept that reality but also identify those things that are within our control.

Unless we consistently try to master our own minds, we risk a loss of control over our lives to fear. We have thus placed ourselves on the spiritual battlefield of life UNARMED.

Choose your goals carefully, and make sure they are really your goals and not someone else's. You just might achieve them!

Hopefully, I have already succeeded in selling you this book! But my real objective is to sell you the idea that you can do more, be happier and take more control of your life and destiny than you might currently realize. A large part of that lies in recognizing and transcending irrational, fear-based behaviors. These fears force us into behaviors that do not serve us and may keep us from taking the risks required to engage in things that might.

I have told you how I got my software development company off the ground. That had been an ardent desire of mine. But guess what? Once I attained it, I realized that it wasn't really what I wanted.

Indeed, I came to see that it was not *my goal* in the first place. It was a goal that had been "sold" to me without my conscious knowledge. Perhaps this was from my upbringing by my very fine parents, or even from movies and romantic TV portrayals of successful entrepreneurs in the corporate world. In any case, I discovered that running that company all but pre-empted my life. It was all I had time to do. It was a real adventure to start the firm, but definitely not to run it day to day.

So I urge you to really examine your goals, even those you might have felt were unreachable. Analyze where that goal came from. Is it your goal? Is it truly what you want? Or has it been sold to you, packaged so to speak, perhaps unconsciously?

Do not let others set your goals for you. Certainly take advantage of knowledgeable counsel. But in the end it is your life, and only you must decide what you want from that one life you have. Realize that every life path decision carries its own risks and its own potential rewards. You must be willing to accept the price that must be paid for your decisions.

The largest fire in Colorado history showed me something unusual about life path decisions. For the first time in history, the Forest Service evacuated everyone from the danger area of Pike National Forest—absolutely everyone. The rangers knew there were a handful of hermits living in abandoned mines and caves, and they evacuated them too.

My wife and I were among those refugees, having been evacuated from our own ranch. In the newspaper I saw grizzled old men, miners and prospectors complete with burros and shovels. They had been living in the forest for years, only rarely coming into town. They could as easily have stepped right out of a time machine from the days of the old Wild West.

They weren't happy about the fire, of course, but they did seem happy in their lives. They had humor and were clearly self-reliant. They were not worrying over their taxes or health insurance payments, either, since they did not have any. They had made an important life decision sometime ago: that they did not want to pay the price that came with these "modern society" things.

I am not recommending this as way of life, of course. I am just pointing out that these prospectors had decided on their own life's goals and were willing to pay the price for their special freedoms.

I perhaps would not change too much about my life decision to create that start-up ATE business either. If I had not taken the chance and done it, then I would always have wondered, "What's it like to start a company and have 28 employees and a few million dollars in revenue running through it?" Now I know what it is like, and I also know that it isn't what I want to do. It just isn't me.

But I did learn important things in that corporate world about managing people and about sales. They are often almost the same. Let me close this chapter by sharing some of the central things about sales that I learned during that period.

As I suggested, sales is really a part of all of our lives no matter what our profession may be. Sales is understanding people's needs and then communicating that to them. Since that is such a fundamental aspect of life itself, I feel it's worth looking at the basic "inner game" of the sales process.

Sales is the job of successfully educating the customer to his needs.

You must *not* try to sell a solution to a person until you first show him that you understand his problem. This may sometimes take work and research, especially in technical sales. For example, you might develop expertise in a given field and understand how that business operates and its special problems. You will then be able to speak with authority and credibility when you define a problem for a customer who is in that industry and who needs your solution.

Having gotten to that point, you can repeat the same cycle of success with the next customer in that same or similar field. Your best sales resource is the testimony of the client whose problem you understood, promised contractually to solve, and then did so beyond his expectations. It is implicit here that you qualify your prospect for your services.

I was in highly technical sales in those earlier days, but the principle above is nearly universal. It even applies to honestly selling used cars. It may take a little thought, but these same concepts apply to selling yourself as a desirable partner in a romantic relationship. Don't you first have to listen to the other person and discover what they want, don't want, or are not ready for? You cannot succeed, at least long term, in forcing a "relationship sale" on someone when you do not understand their needs and expectations, or if you cannot address those needs or expectations, can you?

Sales is primarily the job of overcoming objections.

This is a continuation of educating the client to the nature of his problem and why you can solve it. In my experience there are only three types of objections that you will ever encounter in any sales effort:

1) "I don't need it." This objection arises when the client does not have the problem you think he does and for which you have the solution. Or he may not realize that he has this specific problem yet. You must determine which it is as early as possible. You must pre-qualify your client as needing your service or product and having the ability to pay for it. You must also identify the true decision maker(s) at the outset of the sales effort.

2) "Your solution won't work for me." In this objection the client is saying his circumstances are unique to his operation and that your product or service does not fit his problem. If your solution does not fit their problem, then move on. But some people desire to see their business problems as unique. If this is the case, and yet you see they are not so different, then it is back to Step One again. You must demonstrate that you understand his problem before you can try to sell the benefits of your product or service.

3) "I got a problem all right, and your solution seems like it should work. But there is no hurry to make a decision. After all, we have gotten along this far without your solution." This can be one of the hardest objections to overcome. Demonstrate just how much it is costing them to delay solving the problem and how much more it might cost them in the future. Sometimes you need to remind them of their competition's advantage over them when the competition has already solved the same problem.

Finally, the sales objection that you should never have to face if you are prudent, honest, and careful in your actions is "It sounds good, but SOMEHOW, I JUST DO NOT TRUST YOU." The client may see that you understand his problem. He may even feel that your solution should work, and he wants a solution now. But he feels you have some hidden agenda and that you cannot be trusted to deliver what you contractually promise.

If you encounter this objection, then you have done something terribly wrong and have lost the client's trust. Find out what that mistake was as soon as possible so that you never repeat it with another prospect.

Our character is our fate.

And our character rests primarily on our own personal self-image.

The fundamental premise I have put forth thus far is that for the most part "we are all made of the same clay." For example, the tough guys in the bar had some of the same basic motivations and fears as the prison convict.

Everyone has some of the predatory, animal mind in them too. This is why we must understand and recognize predatory behavior and the "interview" as early as possible anywhere we encounter it.

Even when we examine the criminal and pathological mind of that convict, we can see that his almost incomprehensible behavior—the apparent killing over a cigarette—rests on the extreme end of the same human behavioral continuum. The three tough guys entering the bar were just in a less fearful environment; thus they were not as irrational as the convict killer. But the common element in all these cases is fear of the potential consequence of their actions, or the consequences of their failure to act.

It is easy to see the comparison between the three young guys entering the bar for a fight and the convict who killed over not getting his "props." But what about the IBM executives? What did they really fear, if anything?

The easy answer is that they feared losing control of the negotiations. But the deeper insight is that being in control of the negotiations was part of their self-images as the "big boys from Big Blue." Their necessary "props" (the proper respect due them) was for me to recognize this.

If we attack or challenge the institutions or position that a person's personal self-image is predicated on, then that individual sees us as attacking them *personally*. In such a case we likely have terminated any chance for successful negotiations with them too. They would identify us as the enemy.

I could reason with the three toughs in the bar because I knew what they really wanted, and I was in a position to give it to them without difficulty or risk. I could sell them my peaceful solution to their needs. I was able to negotiate with the IBM senior executive easily because he was already self-confident and had a positive self-image.

Indeed, these are precisely the qualities that will help liberate us from counterproductive, irrational, fear-based behavior. Because the IBM executive was self-confident and rational, it was easy to negotiate with him and to close the deal, which profited us both.

But, could I have negotiated with the convict without giving him his "props" and not paying back that cigarette? Not a chance in hell. The convict had too much at stake. He was also burdened by an uncertain and paranoid self-image. He was dominated by the fear that he might be seen as an acceptable victim to the rest of the prison population if he did not violently retaliate.

We must always try to see what is on the line—that is, what is *at risk* by the other party—in negotiating any deal.

The critical importance of developing an authentically strong personal self-image

Our personal self-image is simply our internal view of who we are and how we fit into the larger human picture of our particular social order. If we have an uncertain personal self-image, we tend to be ruled mainly by fear. We will also make ourselves more vulnerable to being chosen by predators as the victim.

The three guys who came into the bar for a fight had weak personal self-images. They were on a mission to enhance their self-images by getting into a fight and being recognized as non-victims. What kind of self-image do you think the convict had?

In contrast, the IBM executive believed in himself, his abilities and his own self-worth. Note that he was also the happiest and the most successful man of those I have presented.

A person with a weak self-image may become the bully to disguise their fear of their own unworthiness from others. This can be the bully in the barroom or the middle-manager bully at the office.

If our self-image is weak, then the bully will use us as a tool to enhance his own uncertain self-image. Bullies will do this by abusing us in one way or another. This is similar in concept to racial or ethnic bigotry. A look at the racial and ethnic bigot can further illuminate our understanding of the predatory mind and its damaged self-image.

Racial and ethnic bigotry is motivated by fear and a weak self-image.

The racial or ethnic bigot feels deep down, "Maybe I ain't worth much, but at least I am better than that ___." (Fill in the blank with Black, Jew, Whitee, Chink, etc.)

The racial bigot identifies another race as being less than he or even as worthless sub-human flesh. The other race is always clearly identifiable. So it is clear that the bigot is not "one of them." Racial and ethnic bigots find support and common cause with each other. They feed each other's need to feel superior to another racial or ethnic group. This is of course fear-based behavior that flows from their own sense of powerlessness over their own lives.

Similarly, the physical bully or the psychologically abusive bully gets relief from his sense of self-worthlessness and powerlessness by being able to abuse others with impunity.

This shows them that they are at least "better" than the one they abuse. There will always be people around us with weak self-images, and if we do not handle them correctly, they will try to abuse us in one way or another. Indeed the bully seeks out those who lack self-confidence and who have weak self-images. The bully's "interview" that I spoke of earlier is designed to determine if you are a safe victim.

People who value themselves and are confident are not good victims. This is why we must train ourselves to recognize the "interview" as early as possible and to be assertive. Develop a self-image that projects that you are not a safe and suitable victim. Project the idea that they cannot abuse you with impunity.

But in doing this, avoid breaking the four basic rules: 1) Do not insult them; 2) Do not challenge them; 3) Give them the easiest and most face saving exit that you can. Note that none of these things is possible if we 4) display fear during the bully's interview.

An example of dealing correctly with the physical bully

I do not go to bars much these days. But recently I was in a "biker" bar having ridden there on my Harley with my very good friend Crazy Joe Reynolds.

The woman behind the bar had seen both of us there before. My Harley is about 30 years old, and I have been riding that magnificent beast just about that long too. The bike was visible through the doorway of the bar, and the woman behind the bar commented on its age.

In the course of the conversation, I mentioned that I was 53 years old myself. At that point the large "bully" two empty bar stools down from me growled out, "Then you must have lived a pretty soft life."

This, of course, was his "woof" or opening interview. Like a dog barking, the bully will often open his interview with some sort of verbal "woof" like this. Indeed, sometimes the "woof" alone is the interview. I recognized this woof as such.

My objective was to avoid letting this interview go any further and to avoid escalating things by falling into a reactive or aggressive mind-set myself. I turned to him with a slight smile and acted as if I were not overly concerned with his remark and certainly not in fear of him. I said calmly, "Well, maybe some of it wasn't quite as soft as I'd of liked."

He saw that I was not in fear or denial of what was happening or of his real intent either. But surprisingly he left his stool and came over to my stool to loom over me. This was an attempt at physical, body language intimidation. I simply kept my eye on him but showed a relaxed manner. He then actually said, "Most people back down by now."

I was a bit amused at the sheer blatancy of this remark. But I did not show that, since that would provoke his weak self-image. I also felt that there was not going to be any violence so long as I continued to handle him correctly.

I looked him up and down for a second casually and said in a totally relaxed manner, "Well, I can understand that. You're a young, big strong guy. What kind of work do you do?"

I was now giving him the honorable exit, and he took it. He began bragging about how he could handle any type of heavy road-building equipment on the planet. I had given him an alternative method than fighting to display his value and importance. My friend Crazy Joe Reynolds was watching the whole thing and he knew exactly what I was doing. He had seen it many times before. He was silently laughing to himself.

Now, you might think that I was able to handle things because I had been studying and instructing self-defense for years and because I had been a bouncer. In part that may be true. Yet, this kind of knowledge is not taught in martial arts schools, is it?

What I want you to realize is that *you could likely have done the very same thing* and gotten the same results in dealing with this bully. After all, did I have to throw any shots or slip any punches or use any martial arts techniques? Actually, I did use the truest form of martial technique here, because the true art to me is avoiding or resolving conflict without violence.

Do not imagine that this strategy is confined to dealing with a physical barroom bully, either. The bully is the coward afraid of being found out. This is fundamentally true wherever the bully may be. But they can still be dangerous or even fatal to you.

The way I handled this was possible because my personal self-image did not allow others to control my thinking. Another way of saying this: I was not going to allow him to put me into a reactive mind-set.

Again, I am going to use the example of dealing with bullies and tough guys in my bar work to show what this "non-reactive" mind set means. This idea of "non-reactive" mind is also a central theme of Buddhist and Taoist thought.

The non-reactive mind

First, showing no fear is not the same as feeling no fear.

The first three rules of dealing with the bully, in the bar or in the office, implicitly include this fourth rule too: Show no fear. Showing fear is a direct display of the reactive mind. An important tool in learning to show no fear is to develop the ability to engage the non-reactive mindset.

In the first three or four weeks that I began work as a bouncer, I was getting into at least one and sometimes three or four fights a week. My hands hurt and were swollen. I had extensive training and black belts or equivalent in three martial arts, but in those barroom fights, at first I hardly used any of my martial arts techniques. They did not seem available to me. The battles were just too animalistic and brutal.

Basically, all I could do was duck or deflect their blows, grab their shirts, and pound on their heads with punches using my right hand or the edge of my hand or toss them hard into the wall. Later I will discuss why all my martial arts training was not "available" to me *at that point in time*. But for now I want to concentrate on the non-reactive mind.

After four or five weeks I discovered that I was getting into only a third or fewer fights as before. Further, when I was forced to fight, I ended it quickly. I even began to employ some of the most basic martial arts techniques.

What had changed?

The answer is that I recognized and got used to the "hot interview" and threats of the bullies. I was thus liberated from my previously totally reactive mind-set.

Combative patrons would get right in my face shouting that they were going to smash my face into raspberry jam, or that they had money, weren't drunk, were going to have another drink, and there was nothing I could do about it if I didn't want to be bled out right there.

At first, my mind was reactive to this sort of threat. I felt that the guy was challenging my position and my ability and authority to do my job. In my own mind I would say to myself, "Well, this guy isn't going to cool off. He is threatening to beat me senseless and wants a fight, and that's what they are paying me to handle. I guess I have to get to work now."

Can you see that my behavior was fear-based too? It may have been rational fear in this context, but it was fear-based just the same.

To better see this, imagine what my mind-set would have been if I had been totally and absolutely confident that I could defeat this aggressor physically or mentally without being injured myself. Without fear, my options for handling the situation would have been greatly expanded.

But, I was not in that totally confident mind-set, so he made me *think* I had to fight—so there was a fight. I was reacting to his threats, and in this sense he was "controlling" my behavior and my mind.

Yet, while these tough guys always said something like, "I'll stomp your pink ass into the floor," none of them ever did so. In fact, only a handful of those many "woofers" even tried to assault me after making such a threat. So I got used to these threats and developed a non-reactive mind-set to them.

This new attitude gave me a more self-confident presence, and that alone prevented a lot of fights, because the other guy saw that I was not in denial, that I showed no fear, and yet I knew exactly what he had in mind for me. His bully mind was asking the important survival question, "What's wrong with this picture? What am I risking here with this guy?"

But it was most often his frog brain (the part of the brain that is concerned only with survival) that was answering that question, and it said, "Danger, unknown situation. Back off now or you might get us both killed."

I would then give the bully the easiest and most honorable exit possible, and they would take it most times. I was always polite even if in "command voice" mode, and I called them "sir." Yes, a few would go for me anyway, but then *they were in the re-active mind set,* so it was not hard to see their attack coming. It had practically come at my command. They also attacked with a "divided and uncertain mind."

I came to realize that almost anyone could do *most* of my job if they just handled these hostile bullies right. But to do that they would have to let go of their reactive mind-set, display no fear, and think rationally under stress.

We should train ourselves to recognize immediately when someone's actions or words are designed to put us into a reactive mind-set: to control our responses and thinking for their own ends and goals. At the low threat level, such as simple and normal social interaction, their goal might be just to "get our goat."

But their plans may be longer-term than that, too. A person who is intermittently or habitually drawing attention to what they perceive as your failures or shortcomings is trying to mold your self-image into one that is subordinate to their own. It should be apparent that a person who does this has an uncertain or weak self-image.

Again it is the same pattern of thinking found in racial bigotry. The person with less than a positive self-image will find temporary relief by casting another as "less than them."

The basis of our self-image should be inner, not outer.

This means that our feeling of self-worth must be held within ourselves, within our own spirits, and not made overly conditional on external things or on others. For example, if we set a goal for ourselves and then predicate our self-image on attaining that goal, we may be programming ourselves for failure. The chosen goal may be unattainable. But does that mean *we are failures?* No, it does not.

If we predicate who we are on our employment position, then what happens to us and our personal self-image if we lose that position? What happens to us when we retire? Why do you think so many people die shortly after they retire?

We must define and set goals for ourselves. And most certainly we must work to attain goals and measure our progress along the way. Sometimes we need to change our strategies to achieve goals. But we should not let achieving any external goal define who we are or what we are worth.

Our personal self-esteem may fluctuate with circumstances, of course, but our inner feelings of positive self-worth must be fundamentally unconditional. No matter what we do or do not achieve, we must always recognize that we have value and personal dignity.

We must never predicate our self-worth on attaining the goals or employment positions that have been set for us by others, either. Think about this: How many times have you been introduced to someone at a party and the first thing that person asks you is, "And what do you do?" They mean, of course, that what you do for a living primarily defines "who" you are and what you are "worth."

You are much more than how you make a living or support your family.

Our emotions do not depend only on our experiences but also on how we process those experiences.

Human emotions are not like touching a hot stove and jerking our hand away. Emotions are the result of our brains processing an event. In touching a hot stove, there is no mental processing of the event, is there? Pulling away from a hot stove occurs at the frog brain level, not at the self-aware level.

Yet in my martial arts studies, I have seen true masters control and direct (to some degree) what would otherwise be seen as autonomic reflexes. If a person can control their heart rate, pain, and perhaps even bleeding, then is it unreasonable that you can control or redirect your emotional response to events, especially if that control is beneficial to your mental health?

We are continually re-programming our minds, too, through our daily experiences anyway. Yet, we are not often aware of this. A good deal of this re-programming of our mental processing can be called our "self-dialogues." These self-dialogues can be rational and positive, or they can be irrational and self-defeating.

For example, when we say to ourselves, "Judy turned me down for a lunch date. She thinks I am not worthy of her," then part of our subconscious mind may echo, "I am not worthy." Questioning our own worth is self-defeating.

We could process the experience of Judy turning us down for a lunch date by saying to ourselves, "OK, Judy isn't prepared to have lunch with me today, but I think perhaps she will at some other time. Her not wanting to have lunch with me today may have nothing to do with me but with other factors happening in her own life."

This would be a much healthier self-dialogue, because it is based on *hope and self-worth rather than fear.* But being able to feel this way could come only from first having a positive self-image.

You can re-program your mind for greater success, but it takes effort and practice. Nothing is simply given to you. Nor should you feel that the world owes you anything either, not even justice. You must achieve the integrity of your self-worth through your own daily effort. To understand this, it helps to look at technical details of how the human mind works, particularly under stress.

I have a good friend who is an internationally recognized martial arts instructor and a very decent man. He is a Buddhist priest and part of the security entourage for the Dalai Lama of Tibet.

Shidoshi Stephen Hayes told me that he sees Buddhist thought as being a "mind science" rather than a religion. I can definitely see his point. But I think most of us can better grasp these ideas through the western sciences of human physiology and to a lesser extent, human psychology.

CHAPTER REVIEW

1) Human behavior is fundamentally the same in most of us at the deepest level, and it is often motivated by a fear of consequences rather than by hope. We need to examine this in ourselves since irrational fear-based behavior is self-limiting.

2) Fear is often the central motivator of the human predator too, so the predator selects and qualifies their victims before abusing them. Human predators often select their victims

by means of an "interview" to determine if it is safe for them to abuse with impunity. We need to learn to show predators that we are not victims. The process is the same whether in a bar-room with a bully, in the boardroom with a CEO, or with your office manger or co-worker "office bully."

3) We are fundamentally all "sales people," because we all sell something. If conducted honorably, sales is just as honor-able a profession as any other. The art of successful selling is educating the client to his or her needs. But never try to explain a client's needs to them until you have researched them. Do not offer a solution until you can confidently articulate and sometimes document their problem. There are only three basic objections to any sale:

A) Don't need it.

B) It won't solve my problem.

C) There is no hurry to make a decision now, since we have gotten along this far without your solution.

Anticipate how each of these three objections might express themselves in your sales effort and then formulate a plan to de-fuse and overcome them.

4) Our character is our fate, and our character flows from our own self-image. We should not predicate our self-worth on achieving a goal or on any other external basis such as our job title or financial status. We must internalize our strong, per-sonal self-image. It must be made authentic by integrating it into our character. This means that our behavior is congruent with and reinforces and validates our self-image. If you adopt this attitude with sincerity and fidelity then you have built the foundation for a more successful and happy life.

5) We must realize that our emotional responses to interac-tions with others are not autonomic. Any emotional event is in-terpreted through the crystal of our own minds. This occurs both consciously and especially subconsciously. To a signifi-cant extent, this mental processing determines how we will re-spond to others. If our personal self-image is strong and nurtured by our own congruent behavior and character and our intrinsic acknowledgement of our self-worth, then we can

transcend reactive mind. Conversely, the reactive mind is at the mercy of a barrage of external stimuli and other people's agendas. The reactive mind often responds automatically with fear and anger to the words of another. (Fear and anger, by the way, are basically the same thing.) The non-reactive mind is not so easily "hijacked' by another in a negotiation or through fear.

6) You can re-program your mind to respond more productively to interactions with others. We are subconsciously re-programming our minds in some way with each new experience in our daily life. One of the mechanisms that brings this subconscious re-programming to the level of the conscious mind is "self-dialogue." If we make our internal self-dialogues positive, they can maintain and enhance our self-images. But if we engage in negative and irrational self-dialogues, then they turn into self-indictments that tear down our self-esteem and our self-image. That irrational, self-defeating behavior is always rooted in fear.

7) We are not the center of the universe. What others say or feel about us may have much more to do with what is happening in their own lives and with their personal self-images and character than with anything about us.

To understand how you can re-program your mental self-image, it helps to understand first how it is being re-programmed now. That is the subject of our next chapter.

Mind Controls Body

Our brains store information from experiences in two basic and fundamentally different ways. We store information learned under ordinary circumstances in one way and experiences learned under traumatic or more properly termed adrenal states in another very different way.

Information we store in our adrenal minds is more persistent than memories acquired in a non-adrenal state. Adrenal memories are also more directly connected to the neural wiring of our motor control centers and physical senses. This is because action taken in response to a cue that triggers an adrenal memory is in the realm of the "fight or flight" response. This means it bypasses the self-aware, conscious mind. This makes the physical motor response faster in a physical crisis. We don't have to think about it, our *bodies* just do it!

The significance of this is that self-dialogues that affect our personal self-image the most, and on the deeper, less self-aware levels, are usually acquired under adrenal conditions. When our self-dialogues occur under an adrenal state, we are not fully aware of their content. An example would be the self-dialogues you engage in under mild or moderate adrenal events such as your boss yelling at you or even just being too demanding of you.

Or it could be a very dramatic adrenal event such as forcible rape or the horrors of warfare. Once again, the special nature of extreme adrenal memories is at the very heart of Post Traumatic Stress Disorder (PTSD).

In fact, we can automatically react to something a person may say to us in almost the same way we hit that non-existent brake pedal mentioned earlier—that is, without engaging our rational, self-aware minds to evaluate what that person really meant.

If we do not handle stress properly, the formation and revision of our personal self-images can occur without intervention of our self-aware conscious minds. The ideal is to minimize this and to try always to engage our rational thought when we evaluate a stressful experience. Your objective is to re-program your thinking so that you can deal with stress-inducing situations in a more rational, more relaxed and healthy way the next time you encounter one.

When, and if, the rare time comes when the stressful situation is one of "fight or flight" because of immediate physical danger, then your adrenal release is already set up to deal with that with your automatic frog brain responses. Socialization has estranged some of us from these survival instincts to the point that they may nearly lie dormant in some persons. But survival instincts are still present in all of us, and they are easily brought to the surface with a real world traumatic experience or by proper scenario based adrenal stress training.

I can say from experience that these instincts are so primeval that they can be elicited and resurrected in almost anyone, and in a surprisingly short period. I have seen this occur many times at RMCAT in a single weekend of adrenal stress training.

An example of training for failure in the martial arts world

While this is an example from my martial arts experience, I feel that it applies almost universally. It is said that we fight as we train, but let's also realize that we think as we experience—that is, we think as we experience the world and the people about us.

Once when I was in California teaching an adrenal stress scenario based self-defense class, I was invited by some sheriff's deputies to their home for a few drinks. One of the deputies was a highly ranked practitioner of a particular nerve-striking art. He demonstrated his art by sparring with his student, who was also a deputy. Both of them were large, strong men.

In watching them spar, I saw a classic case of an instructor training the student to fail. The instructor had trained the student such that when they sparred, the student was driven into a totally reactive mind-set.

It was like Pavlov's dogs, which were conditioned to salivate when a bell rang. But in this case, the student had been conditioned to recoil and brace for the pain of impact from the instructor's nerve strike. The student winced and recoiled *before* he was even hit. He had been sensitized to anticipate the pain, and he braced and stiffened at seeing the strike coming.

To my way of thinking, he could have just as easily been trained to counter or slip the strike. But the instructor was either unaware of what he was doing, or an uncertain self-image needed the external "prop" of displaying that he could inflict pain on this physically large student at will. I regret to say that I feel it was mostly the latter.

The point is that we can be conditioned to react on a visceral frog brain level to the words and actions of others. We can, for example, be unknowingly trained to respond aggressively to what appears as a verbal attack, while the other person was only making a neutral observation. This type of knee jerk response is a defense mechanism that can develop inside us without our conscious knowledge.

What we are really doing in such cases is rushing to defend the "holes" in uncertain portions of our self-image. We often store a few verbal "triggers" in our pre-consciousness, and they are then cemented into our self-aware mind by our own negative self-dialogues.

For example, suppose a person feels that their ability in some area is poorly regarded by others (co-workers, mate, friends etc). Let's suppose this is their ability to follow directions and find an address. Imagine that they are driving the car and the others present are conscious of the driver's self-perceived inadequacy to find an address.

In this case, the driver is cued up to verbally defend against the slightest remark by anyone who suggests that they are not heading in the right direction. Let's see how this might play out:

Passenger: "Ok, that's 7th Street. We will be coming up on Bellview soon."

Driver (shouts back with hostility): "I know! We'll get there! Just relax!"

The passenger was actually reassuring the driver that they were on course, but the driver was cued up to hear a complaint about their inability to follow directions. Consequently, the driver heard that and responded with a knee-jerk reflex.

In fact, the driver might respond similarly to anything the passenger said as the driver was "prepped" and "cued" to defend this self-perceived "hole" or weakness in their own self-image because of their "incompetence" in this area of following traffic directions.

This can even lead to an escalation of miscommunication if the passenger then objects:

"Damn, I only said we were passing 7th Street. Don't be so damn sensitive!"

Driver: "I am not sensitive! It's just that you are always trying to put me down when I'm following a map. You are trying to make me think you're so much smarter than me. Well listen to me...!"

Remember the famous line by Strother Martin (the Southern chain gang warden) in the film *Cool Hand Luke*? "What we have here is ... a failure to communicate."

Most of us can recall similar situations where everything seemed to be going fine, and then a wrong word set off a heated argument and an exchange of mutual recriminations. Most likely the event occurred during a stressful event: for example, going to a wedding, a funeral, or an important meeting. In each case, we allowed our reactive mind to dominate over rationality.

Our brains can be taught at a near subconscious level to do remarkable things.

Thanks to your early teachers, you learned to read. In fact, now you read fluently. I want to demonstrate that you read at a near subconscious *processing level.* Your brain recognizes whole words rather than just the individual sequence of letters that make them up. Try reading the following paragraph:

"Aoccdring to rseheearch at Cmabridge Uinervtisity, it deosn't mttaer in what order the ltters in a word are. The only imporetant thing is taht the frist and lsat ltteer be in the rghit pclae. The rset can be a total mses and msot can still raed it just fine."

Just as your brain has learned read the above even though the words are butchered, you can learn to re-program elements of your preconscious and even subconscious mind. In time you can learn to do this to the point that it reduces stress and allows you to employ rational rather than irrational reflexive and re-active thinking.

Cascade failure of the self-image: an extreme case

Some personalities are prone to non-productive thinking, negative self-dialogue and miscommunication. But I feel that almost anyone, with knowledge and effort, can modify their thought processes and how they internally evaluate an experience. We cannot control the world, but we can develop positive, conscious control over how we feel about the world. That means feeling hope rather than fear or resignation to some self-perceived uncontrollable fate.

Again, I will use an extreme example to underscore this principle. We might call this the "cascade failure" phenomena. Here is how this negative self-dialogue might play out:

"Judy won't have lunch with me. Why should she? Patty and Julie didn't either. No woman is interested in me, and there is nothing that I can do about that. I'm just not good enough for them. I'll never find a woman who wants me. I hate this damn job too! What is there left to live for anyway? I might as well be dead. I might as well shoot myself right now!" Click, bang!

OK, an extreme, compressed example. But don't you imagine that this scene has played itself out, right up to that fatal pull of the trigger?

The excessive need for approval from others

We all want approval, but approval from others should never become more important than our own self-approval. We must resist allowing others to detract from our internal, positive self-image. If we do not see ourselves as winners, we won't be winners. If we think of ourselves as losers, we are losers.

The real trick sometimes is just determining what it is that you really want and need to "win" and why. A person who has an excessive need for approval has placed him or herself at the mercy of others in one way or another. In my experience, there are three basic personality types that are dominated by this excessive need for the approval of others.

The first is, ironically, the Perfectionist. Another we might call the People Pleaser, and the third is the Enabler.

The Perfectionist feels that he or she must be perfect in everything. They cannot tolerate rejection. In fact, a perfectionist often defines himself or herself as being their work. They are often true workaholics.

The perfectionist's demand for approval manifests itself in devaluing those who won't give their approval. The perfectionist may even demand that others not just approve of them but admire them. They cannot accept their own flaws, so they tolerate even less the flaws of others.

Ironically, the perfectionist sets himself or herself up for failure. Nobody is perfect, and so he or she has set unobtainable goals for themselves. The perfectionist may have success in business or work, but they tend to alienate everyone around them with their demanding behavior and rigid self-rules.

Perfectionists do not have a realistic, stable and strong personal self-image. It is externally based on getting things done. This is why they cannot tolerate flaws in themselves particularly when another expresses it. Perfectionists see criticism as a personal attack. The perfectionist may also feel that others are responsible for his own failures.

One perfectionist I know is a veterinarian. He works constantly and he is very good at his profession. But he is also a very driving, demanding, classic type "A" personality. A friend mentioned this to him and his responded, "Hell yes I'm a type 'A.' They are the ones that get things done!"

His problem in his rural veterinary practice is that he is a "one man band" as he can't retain an employee for more than three or four weeks. He is just too driving and demanding.

The People Pleaser also feels an excessive need for approval from others. The people pleaser seeks approval by keeping everybody happy. They accept responsibility for the happiness of everyone around them. This leads to an over-developed sense of pseudo-empathy. They think everyone else is as sensitive to the approval of others as they are, and they fear disapproval.

The person with a strong personal self-image *will always have a strong sense of true empathy* for others but not to the degree that they mistakenly feel responsible for the happiness of everyone around them. Again, such an attitude would be programming ourselves for failure.

Ultimately, all cruelty comes from pain and weakness and fear, while all true empathy and compassion can come only from strength—not physical strength of course, but a strong personal self-image. From this can flow spiritual strength. This is the kind of spiritual strength that permits rational self-sacrifice for others.

The Enabler has an excessive need for approval but generally from a specific individual or even a specific organization rather than everyone around them as with the people pleaser. This may be a spouse or lover or even just a close friend they have come to depend on. The enabler often excuses abusive behavior in exchange for the abuser's approval and acceptance. The spouses of alcoholics are often enablers of some stripe. Women who remain in physically or psychological abusive relationships are often classic enablers. They also have the self-image of a victim. Their abusers abuse them because they let them do so. This is the essence of the enabler.

Cults: the institutionalized enablers of human weakness and fear

A special type of enabler personality joins cults. A cult is an organized mechanism for the exploitation of human weakness and fear. A cult serves the cult itself rather than the cult members. If it is a cult of personality—and most are—then the cult serves that particular personality and secondarily the entourage of their "inner circle."

Every cult serves the cult leaders. Those leaders are very sophisticated and successful predators. The cult selects victims the same way any other predator does. They look for persons with incomplete, uncertain or traumatized self-images.

From Charlie Manson to the Reverend Moon, the cult leader is a master at predation: a master of manipulation and ferreting out a person's fears and weakness and then exploiting them.

Habits can be hard to break

The perfectionist, the people pleaser and the enabler all deal with significant anxiety for the approval of others. They have *externalized* the basis of their own self-image. When we have anxiety and conflict, we have some level of adrenal flow. Things practiced or learned under adrenal stress, as we have seen, can become automatic responses.

Consequently, the personal behavior and conflict resolution methodology for all three of these personalities (though expressed differently) can become ingrained into them almost automatically. It becomes so habitual that they do not realize they are doing it. They will often deny they are doing it. The behavior becomes part of their survival modus operandi, especially under stress, in order to maintain their uncertain self-image.

They often do not see that their strategy is not working, because it is not fully directed by their self-aware minds. So they continue the same habitual self-defeating behavior. It is challenging to communicate effectively with such personalities. But it helps to recognize which of these "personality directions" the person you may be dealing with is primarily manifesting.

In time the cult leader can convince himself or herself—that is, actually reprogram and rewire their own mind—that they are what they claim to be (i.e. a Messiah or the Savior or even God). This shows the power we have over re-wiring our own thinking and perception of reality.

A cult leader is the master predator. They exploit and destroy with their knowledge of re-programming minds. But as with any "tool" or knowledge, this power can be used for honorable purposes too.

Discover the automatic responses you have developed to personal conflicts.

One of the techniques I found very useful in maintaining or reducing body weight was to write down everything I ate each day. Once I did this, I saw that I was eating more calories and fats than I had realized. I also became more conscious about how much I ate, what I ate, and even when I ate. This same technique can help to reduce negative self-dialogues as well.

Do this at the end of the day or during work hours, if you can: When you have a stressful exchange of words with someone, write down what they said and how you responded verbally and physiologically. Do this as quickly after the event as possible.

Then later on examine how rational your response and your first analysis was. Perhaps it was perfectly rational and appropriate to the situation at hand. But like those hidden calories I was eating, there may be more to the situation than you first realized. Under stress, most of us are not as rational and self-aware as when we are not under stress. We have all said or done things under stress and/or anger that later we regretted and in hindsight saw as irrational, haven't we? I know I have.

Here is another perhaps familiar example of a miscommunication and avoidable conflict. Your mate is often late getting ready to go to dinner or to see a movie or to meet friends. In the past this caused an argument. That argument elicited some adrenal flow. Hence, the response of arguing over punctual preparedness has been sensitized into you and at the cue that your mate is going to be late. Indeed, it may be just your commitment to being somewhere at a given time that cues up this potential "argument" response.

The man looks at the clock and says, "Well, we will be fine. It's only six o'clock now."

But the woman, conditioned as noted, hears this and but does not hear the *meaning*. She explodes since she was pre-consciously waiting for the cue of her mate complaining that they were going to be late. Hence, that is what she hears in his words.

She yells back, "OK damn it! If you can't wait for me just go by yourself."

To her, his words are pressuring her to hurry up. He is just mystified at her reaction to his simply stating what time it was. This is a classic form of miscommunication based on one person's expectation of an adrenal cue from another. Writing down what was said, what was "heard" and what then transpired can help put us in touch with these miscommunications. You and your mate might even find this practice amusing. Humor is such an essential emotional survival quality, and how sad our lives would be without it.

Amplification, rigid self-rules, and self-fulfilling prophecies

The above examples are easily spotted negative self-dialogue modes that you might identify when you start to record your behavior on paper. You will become more aware of these behaviors in other people too, and that can help you prepare, anticipate, and deal with others more effectively.

Amplification is distorting the magnitude of the conflict or problem we face. We have presented one example of amplification in our "cascade failure" scenario of a very negative self-dialogue. Judy turned down the individual for a simple lunch date, and he amplified this to mean that he would never find any woman to love him. That spiraled his thinking into his dissatisfaction with his job, and then he blew his brains out because he decided his life was not worth living anymore.

Again, this is an extreme case cited to emphasize the point. So let me give you an example of a more common stressful situation that I sometimes have to deal with. Very likely some of you have also.

Amplification of the anxiety-producing situation

I do not often eat in fast food places, but very rarely I have too.

I do not wait in line well either.

Here is the scenario. There are three groups of people ahead of me. The group at the counter is deciding what they want to order *while standing at the counter*. They are teenagers who even converse with each other casually as I, and others, wait: "Oh try the Chicken chunks...did you hear what Bobby actually said to Susan yesterday?" Sometimes they change their order after they have told the person at the counter what they want. They seem oblivious that others are waiting in line.

My Irrational, Amplified Self-Dialogue: "Why do such people live? They act like time is infinite and they will live forever! Why the hell don't they know what they want before they get to that damn counter? They don't give a damn about wasting my time. And Jesus Christ on a bicycle, I'll bet the next group in front of me will be just as stupidly unprepared and take all day too! They should all die spitting blood!"

OK, I think a good fantasy life and humor are healthy, so I confess that sometimes I allow myself to entertain these mental self-dialogues, somewhat irrational as they maybe. However, if I am reciting this self-dialogue in a light-hearted way, then it is not so irrational really. In such cases, I am using humor to help me get through the stressful situation.

But sometimes I find myself short-tempered with people who make me wait in line. Most times if I let this anger-based, irrational, amplification type self-dialogue go unchecked, then I will turn and leave the fast food place at once. You cope with a situation or you get out of it.

But odds are that I will then drive to another fast food place and experience a similar wait. I end up wasting more time this way, but to be honest, I may still feel better about it because I feel more in control!

Here is how I try to program myself to think more rationally in this situation so that it is less stressful for me and I don't waste even more time searching for another fast food place without a line. I mentally rehearse this *before* I have to wait in a line. I try to make a game of it with myself.

My Rational Self-Dialogue: "Ok, I have a group of adolescents here and they are having a good time, even though it is partly at my expense. This does aggravate me, but this is also one of my behavioral problems that I am trying to work on. I am just going to take a deep, abdominal breath and relax myself. None of this is personal anyway, because these kids are oblivious. But they will eventually place their order, and then I have just two more people to go. It may seem like a long time now, but in reality it will be just a handful of minutes. I can handle that. Now relax, breath and let go. There is nothing really at stake here."

Overly rigid rules for life

I do not think I am the type who has a rigid set of rules in their head about how everything should work and how everybody should act. But do you see that the underlying idea I had in my irrational self-dialogue at the fast food place is pretty close to having a rigid, fixed rule for everybody's behavior? Specifically, that rule would be: "People should always be ready with their order when they come to the counter, goddamn it!"

We just cannot expect people to follow our personal set of rules for how the world should work. To do so is to set ourselves up for anxiety and inner turmoil.

A common "rigid rule of life" we might observe is "Everybody has to be on time all the time!" I demanded this of my students when I was a high school teacher. That was appropriate and rational behavior in that context. But what if I were locked into this "rigid rule of life" when I sat waiting for those executives from IBM in that Denver office? Then I might have worked myself up into such a state while waiting for them that I could not have handled them successfully and rationally in terms of my own objectives. I might have even have reproached them for being late!

Do you see how all this is related? It is all one great reactive and interconnected package of human dynamics. Reproaching the IBM people for being late would be attacking them personally as I would be challenging the very identity upon which their self-images were partially predicated. It would have been a negotiational disaster for which I would not likely have been able to recover. I would have scuttled my own ship!

We should examine our hearts and our intellects for the rigid self rules of life that we might be carrying, or might I say, burdening ourselves with. A rigid rule of life is irrational when it does not serve us. Expecting people to always act the way we think they should is not realistic. Expecting people to be always on time or always ready with their food order at a fast food place is just not realistic. It does not serve us, because we will encounter cognitive dissonance and anger when we run into those who violate our rigid rule of life.

On the other hand, of course, a few rigid rules of life *are rational ones.* I, for example, have a rigid rule of life that says nobody will force entry into my home on a mission of violence without being met with deadly force. This is rational thinking, as it serves my wife and me. My hope is that I never have to put this rigid rule into action, but maintaining this rule helps me in psychologically preparing myself before the fact should an intruder force entry into my home.

Resigning oneself to self-fulfilling prophecies

Perhaps this concept is best described by a joke I heard as a child:

A salesman gets a flat tire in the countryside at night. He discovers that he has no jack to change the tire. As a salesman he has had an unsuccessful day dealing with the country people he is trying to sell farm equipment to. He is walking down an empty road at night away from his disabled car when he sees a farmhouse a few miles away. Here is how his irrational self-dialogue goes:

"These dumb hicks. They can't see the value of my equipment because they're just too damn stupid! They think they can get along just the way they always have and don't need anything new or improved. They're suspicious of strangers and city people, down right paranoids. Hell, if I go up to that farmhouse to ask for a jack they might shoot at me. Those kind of ignorant bastards probably don't even have a jack anyway!"

After walking a few miles the salesman reaches the farmhouse. He stops a moment and yells out from the road: "OK you goddamn hick bastards, keep your goddamn jack!" He then walks away.

Compare this to the guy who thought that because Judy would not have lunch with him, no woman would ever want him. It is the same thing. His negative self-dialogue could easily become a self-fulfilling prophecy, too. Like the irate salesman, his attitude would direct his behavior such that his prediction that he would never find a woman would become a reality. We cannot allow ourselves to think in this fashion. It never serves us.

Many times the lack of approval from others has nothing to do with us, but with their own state of mind.

Just as the salesman's disapproval of the people in the farmhouse had nothing to do with the attitudes of the people in the farmhouse, recognize that some of the disapproval that you receive has nothing personally to do with you either.

Suppose a man comes home to his wife, and he expects her to have dinner ready that night as previously agreed. He has had a very stressful day, and when he gets home his unresolved hostility transfers to his wife's failure to get the "right damn mustard for these burgers!"

This situation can easily escalate if both partners do not engage their rational rather than their reactive minds. That escalation can even lead to shouting at one another about all their various complaints.

The husband has amplified the "mustard problem" in his own mind and then projected it onto his wife. The wife should see that his anger has little to do with her. But it has a lot to do with how *his* day went. However, if she internalizes this disapproval into her self-image, then she will be enabling her husband's abusive and irrational behavior.

She would do better by letting him explain and thus partially dissipate his anger over how his day went. But if she has had a bad day too, she should not totally suppress her own emotions either. She might remind him, "Honey, I work too and my day has not gone any better than apparently yours has. I fixed this meal and I'm sorry we don't have the mustard you like, but let's just sit down and try to have as pleasant a dinner as we can. Can we agree on that?"

This approach is not only rational but also applies the previously outlined basic canons of salesmanship: She is asking for an agreement.

Why we need to recognize dysfunctional personality types and negative self-dialogues

What is the practical value in knowing about perfectionists, people pleasers and enablers and how they think? The value lies in knowing something about whom we are dealing with so that we might deal with them more productively. Alternatively, we might see that we just need to avoid them altogether.

Remember the convict "cigarette" killer? This extreme example is one of the personality types that you cannot negotiate with if you were the one who did not pay back the cigarette.

Yet please understand that the perfectionist, people pleasers and enablers all exist on a very long continuum too.

When we first encounter a person in almost any setting, it is often useful to initially listen more than we speak. In this way we obtain information and determine what kind of personality direction we are dealing with. We can thus avoid unintentionally alienating them at the very outset. First impressions are indeed important.

Hopefully, though, you will discover that you are dealing with a self-confident person with a positive self-image. These are the easiest and most productive people to work and play with. But don't look for perfection in anyone; it just isn't out there.

People who try to detract from your personal self-image do not serve you.

You should think about what persons are in your life space that you are better off without because they drain too much of your life's energy to maintain a relationship with. These persons I speak of are the ones who habitually force you to engage in negative self-dialogues.

Of course, we all have at least some small measure of all these negative personality qualities in ourselves too, just as we all have some part of the predator in us. We must recognize and accept this reality. If we do not, we are only fooling ourselves and handicapping our self-awareness.

It is once again a question of the quality of our own character. This is why our character is indeed our fate. We forge our character through behavior, self-control and personal integrity. Hence, it is through these same methods that we can also forge our own fate. We cannot change our thinking or behavior until we honestly face what that behavior is.

Part of the mirror we use to see ourselves imperfectly reflects the faces of others—that is, their reaction to our own actions and words. Are we succeeding in communicating with them? Are we getting closer to our goals with them? Have we defined just what our goals—personal or business—are in the relationship with them?

Yet, as we examined earlier, we need to avoid putting an irrational value on the world's opinion of us too. After all, we are the only ones who have to live in our own skins, so it is we who must make that a comfortable dwelling for ourselves.

Sometimes we need to do a cost/benefit analysis of the situation and ask ourselves rational questions. How much does this person's opinion really mean to me and why? What do I need to do to maintain the relationship? Is it worth it? How will I see this situation two months or two years from now?

You might have to take a serious look to see if you are an enabler of the other person in the relationship's problems. And you have to examine whether it is the other way around too.

There is no true "killer instinct" in us. It is only survival instinct, and we need to get in touch with it to reclaim our mental wholeness.

Many of us have been socialized to feel estranged from our survival instincts. These are not just our physical survival instincts but also the survival mindset that recognizes when we are being "prepared" or "interviewed" for victim.

I feel that people who have never had to engage this survival mindset are handicapped when dealing with today's predators, be they physical threats on the street or psychological ones in the office or even at home.

These survival instincts are inside us all. If therefore we do not develop internal communication with them, we cannot control them very well. In fact, under stress and crisis, they can control us.

We must squarely face these survival instincts and our inner fears to better integrate knowledge of them into our self-aware consciousness. Then they can become *tools* for us to use rather than "vestigial organs" that can later become malignant like an inflamed appendix.

It is the adrenal reaction that so reliably elicits the frog brain's survival instincts. But if one is introduced to these instincts in their first life and death crisis, or even in what the body perceives as such, then one can hesitate. They can choke and freeze up. They are caught in limbo between their rational self-aware consciousness and their frog brain's imperative to act.

The training we provide at RMCAT has shown me a great deal about how this survival instinct works and how it can be elicited and actualized in anyone. It is part of everyone's deeper psychological makeup. When people experience that reality, they become a more balanced and much stronger person.

In women the survival instinct gets its most powerful expression in their maternal instincts.

Physiological effects of adrenal stress

First let's acquaint ourselves with the basic physiological effects of the adrenal rush:

1) Tunnel Vision: One's field of vision narrows and tunnels into the perceived threat.

2) Auditory Exclusion: The hearing tends to shut off.

3) Loss of fine motor control: Often only gross motor functions are possible under the adrenal state.

4) Tai-chi-Psyche: Everything seems to move in slow motion.

5) Increased heart rate, blood pressure and respiration.

Virtually every person in our RMCAT class experiences all of these during the course, so I see them as almost universal. They vary only in the degree that they are present and in the degree that they prevent someone from responding in the most effective and appropriate fashion to a given adrenal stress-eliciting scenario.

For example, tunnel vision. If a person draws a weapon on us with malevolent intent, we tend to tunnel our visual field into that weapon alone. The knife, for example, is all we see and not his companion or a way to escape the situation.

We can react to hot words or verbal attack and even constructive criticism with tunnel vision. We see only a verbal attack but not the larger picture—what motivates those words and their real content. By "tunneling" into the hot words, we can't see how to process the information in a more authentic, beneficial and rational way.

When I was robbed at gunpoint

As a side note, let me relate a personal story about tunnel vision under the stress of an armed robbery.

It was my first experience with armed robbers. It occurred when I was running my liquor store many years ago. Two men were coming into the store. Before they even came through the door, I saw them and knew something was not right. I was listening to my frog brain.

I looked at my pistol under the counter, and my frog brain somehow told me, "Don't go for that gun now." In the next instant, the larger man came through the door. He stepped aside revealing a smaller man with a sawed-off shotgun pointed directly at me.

Needless to say, this was a high adrenal moment for me.

Yet, I had already dealt with adrenal situations involving my possible death before. That is the key, to become conditioned to performing under adrenal stress before we face a crisis.

I said, "OK guys you can get the money and be out of here in seconds, and you don't have to rap up a murder charge to do it." I was trying to sell them on the idea of not killing me. I suppose this was one of the most important sales of my life.

The larger guy, which I called the Gopher, passed in front of the shotgun man as the Gopher made his way behind the counter. As the Gopher did this, I noticed that the shotgun man raised his weapon a moment to bring his partner out of the line of fire. I concluded that the shotgun man did not want to see his partner shot.

I was concerned that they had not attempted to disguise themselves. I knew that this might have been because they did not intend to leave me alive as a witness.

My gut told me to take the chance when it came and act, because in this case a compliance survival strategy might be a fatal mistake.

The shotgun man ordered me out from behind the counter as he picked up my .45 automatic pistol from near the register. I figured that he ordered me outside of the register island because he was concerned that I might have other weapons behind the counter.

But there was only a narrow space between the register island and the beer and wine coolers. If I stayed in that narrow space when the Gopher came out from behind the counter, he would have to pass in front of me and the shotgun once again. I was praying that the shotgun man did not order me to come closer to the counter as that would allow the Gopher to pass behind me, giving the gunman a free field of fire with his scattergun.

The Gopher was around six-foot-one and 220 pounds or more. He wore a long, black leather coat. As he came out from behind the counter with a paper bag of cash from the register, he passed between me and the muzzle of the shotgun. That was what I was waiting for. That was my chance.

I grabbed the Gopher's leather coat and twisted it to remove the slack from it (as in my former judo training). This gave me an iron grip on the Gopher. I knew that if he broke away, the shotgun man would be free to shoot me. But for now, since the Gopher was so much larger than I, he made a good shield. I knew that if the gunman fired, the buckshot would not penetrate the Gopher to hit me. I also resolved that if a shotgun blast turned the Gopher into a corpse in the next second, that I would martial all my strength to continue to hold him up as a shield.

After I grabbed the Gopher's leather coat, the shotgun man became frantic. He tried to move to where he could fire on me in that narrow passageway without hitting his partner. I found myself moving the Gopher like he was a rag doll to keep him between me and the shotgun. I suppose a videotape of this might seem funny or even ridiculous. I was no more than eight feet from the guy with the shotgun. He kept jerking his sawed-off weapon about trying to get a clear shot at me.

As I held the Gopher as a shield, I moved toward the door to the backroom of my liquor store. Then came the critical moment: I had to use both hands to open the door and get into the backroom. If I made it that far I could slam and lock the door shut. But to do that I'd have to release my grip on the Gopher!

The shotgun man had moved very close at the moment I reached the closed door to the back room, so I shoved the Gopher into him with everything I had, almost knocking both of them down. By the time the shotgun man recovered a fraction of a second later, I had spun into the backroom.

Most likely the armed robbers had no interest in going into the back room to find me as they probably suspected that I had another gun back there. Knowing how adrenal stress can distort one's sense of time, as I waited in the backroom for the robbers to leave I counted off the seconds—"One thousand and one, one thousand and two..."

I wanted to wait 45 seconds before I kicked the door back open. I wanted to give the crooks just enough time to leave before I got to the only phone in the store, the one behind the counter island.

When I hit 45 seconds I kicked open the door and used the wall and doorframe as cover. This action drew no gunfire but I still could not be sure that they were gone. After all, they had behaved like real pros to this point. I searched for movement in the reflection of the glass whiskey bottles on the shelf outside the backroom. There was none.

I threw out a bottle of Schnapps, and it crashed to the floor. There was no response. I took a deep breath, barreled out from the backroom, and ducked behind the counter. They were gone. I dialed 911 and said to the dispatcher, "Armed robbery, Curve Liquors in Lafayette, two black men one armed with sawed-off shotgun, the other with a .45 auto pistol, likely headed north on 287..."

The police arrive

When the cops arrived some five minutes later, they asked me for a description of the two men. I told them that one was over 6 feet tall, 220 pounds or so with a scar on his right wrist. The other was 5'8" and about 145 pounds. The smaller man was armed with a Mossberg Model 500 pump action shotgun cut down to about 24 inches overall. The bluing on the gun was very worn on the bottom of the slide tube. He had a spider tattoo in the outside webbing of his right hand.

As I continued my description, I noticed that the two police officers were looking at me in amazement. I said, "What?"

They told me that most times when they ask these questions, such as what did the weapon look like, the storeowners say, "It was the biggest gun I ever saw!" This is due to their tunneling into the weapon under the adrenal rush such that it fills their entire field of vision and appears much larger than it really is.

Let me point out that the armed robber predators apparently counted on these adrenal effects to prevent their victims from giving a description of them. I make this conclusion because it was later discovered that the robbers that night were on their 18th liquor store robbery, and they had never worn disguises in any of those robberies!

But this time the police had a good description and a quick 911 call. The local sheriff, the state police and the city police were all involved in the chase and capture. As one detective told me later, "The world caught up with them."

Do you see how the predator knows human psychology and some of the subjects we are discussing in this book? The predator uses that knowledge for criminal purposes. You can use this knowledge too, but I hope for the higher purpose of your self-actualization and perhaps the actualization of others.

The criminal predator feels adrenal-based fear too during the commission of his crime.

I have interviewed a good number of armed robbers, murderers and violent drug dealers over the years. Most of these interviews were done on videotape in and outside of prison. The liquor store robbery I have just related brings one of those interviews to mind and illustrates how even the armed robber with shotgun in his hands is experiencing fear. I will quote directly from the interview of this armed robber and methamphetamine addict who specialized in robbing large grocery stores in the late sixties and early seventies:

"Well, when you get to robbing and cowboying like that and you got everybody on the floor and your shotgun on um' and some of um' are yelling 'please don't shoot me' or whatever, well it scares the Jesus out of them, or into them. (He laughs.) But if you got that guy whose lying there calm, maybe with his head peeking around a bit, well he's the one you are worried about. You see, he's thinking. (He laughs again.)"

It is clear that this armed robber is well aware of both his internal environment (how he is responding) and the external environment (how his victims are responding). He is especially aware of how the adrenaline complex hijacks the victim's rationality, allowing the robber to completely control the victim by fear of being shot. The people on the floor have likely never imagined that this might happen to them.

If the predator fails to instill fear into one of his victims, even though the predator is holding the shotgun, then that is the guy the predator is most worried about. The predator is concerned about those he cannot fully intimidate and control.

Once again, not every predator out there is the criminal holding a scattergun on you. Some predators will be sitting behind a large oak desk and wearing a three-piece suit when you have to negotiate with them.

The same rules apply, though. Even the three-piece-suited predator will be concerned with the person that he or she cannot fully intimidate to their satisfaction, and that can mean that they will really have to negotiate with you.

Auditory exclusion

Has someone ever yelled at you but your mind no longer heard or understood them, though you could see their lips move and their face contort? This is called auditory exclusion from the adrenal pump you are experiencing.

In fact, in police shooting incident reports, an officer may say that they did not hear the sound of the shots they fired but that they only felt the recoil of the gun in their hand. They may be mistaken about how many shots they fired as well; they will often underestimate the number fired. This is the result of auditory exclusion brought about by adrenal stress.

Loss of fine motor control

Fine motor control involves skills like typing. Many martial arts techniques demand fine motor skills and balance. This is why they can fail in a real fight. The martial artist is overcome by the adrenal rush and has no access to their martial techniques. This is because the techniques depend on fine motor control, which can evaporate under adrenal stress. They have practiced their martial training without being under true adrenal stress. Hence, their martial skill is not in their frog brains, and it is the frog brain that is in control during a real fight.

At first this is what I experienced as a bouncer, too. Though I had ranking belts in three martial arts, all I could do until I got accustomed to the adrenal stress was to hold my assailants by the collar and bang away on them with my right hand!

Seeing things moving in slow motion

If you have ever been in an automobile accident, perhaps you recall that when the car turned in front of you, everything seemed to move in slow motion until the impact. If you were a passenger in the car, you may have thought that the driver had plenty of time to brake or turn, but they did not.

Under adrenal stress, the brain, in narrowing the field of vision (tunnel vision) and reducing or eliminating the auditory pathways (auditory exclusion) frees up processing power for the visual centers. This is why things seem to move more slowly, because you are seeing them "faster."

This can be a very powerful survival mechanism, and that is why we have been given this survival-enhancing adrenal response. But if we are not conditioned to the adrenal response through experience with this altered state, we are often overcome by it, at least the first few times out.

In a real life-threatening situation, you may get only one time out. That is where many well-practiced martial artists fail in an actual self-defense encounter, too. They have to do everything right under high adrenal stress. But they have not trained under that condition. They then have to achieve this transition from martial arts to the real thing their very first time out.

As a bouncer, a few times when a tough guy was "woofing" on me, it appeared that I was listening to a tape recording being played at too slow a speed. Then it would appear as if the belligerent patron was moving so slowly that he was underwater.

At that point I would see his slow-motion attack, and there was plenty of time to defend or even pre-empt and check his attack. Through repeated adrenal exposures, my body learned to use my frog brain as evolution had intended.

I find it intriguing that the 15th century Samurai Musashi wrote, "Have correct mind...and there will be plenty of time to get things done."

Even serious martial arts training can fail under the high adrenal stress of an actual attack.

My staff and I see flailing and even worse from young, strong, well-trained and talented martial artists in our RMCAT scenarios. You might ask how we can really adrenalize someone by pretending to assault them or by verbally abusing or threatening them?

The answer is easy, and it works every time with *anyone.* Physiologically we are all made of the same clay. We have an expression for this among my staff: "The body does not know the difference."

When we present authentic cues of malevolence in word, body carriage and action, and all of this is congruent, a person leaves their self-aware mind and enters their adrenal frog brain mind. The adrenal mind is not capable of self-aware, complex analytical thought, so it cannot distinguish the scenario from reality. The only reality that the adrenal mind knows is fight or flight.

The martial artist's problem is that he or she has rarely trained under hard adrenal stress. The closest they may have come to this is in a full-contact tournament. But in that arena they are right in their element, like a fish in water. They also know the opponent has no real intent to injure or kill them.

They can remain largely in their self-aware, tactical mind in the prize ring. They can employ fine motor skill movements in those tournaments. The ring has safety rules. The contestants know that they will face only one person, there will be no weapons, and there is even a referee to stop the event if it gets too dangerous. Of course, this is how a sport must be conducted.

Perhaps the most important difference between sport in the ring and an actual confrontation that may lead to a fight and injury or death is that in the prize ring, both people already know *why they are there.* They are both psychologically prepared for a fight. They both have some level of confidence that they will prevail.

The real world outside the prize ring is not like that. Real predators out there will often not even attack if they perceive that you are psychologically prepared for battle. Consider the bully I dealt with in that biker bar. He did not attack because he saw I was psychologically prepared for this and I showed no fear. Then I gave him an easy, face-saving way out, and he took it.

How assertiveness applies to the workplace

Consider your work environment. Suppose you are a woman (or I suppose a man too now days), and you know that a manager or other "superior" is approaching your desk to make an inappropriate sexual remark.

As he or she approaches your desk, stand up and look coldly but calmly right into their eyes. You do this because you already know their intentions. Do you think they will continue with their plan? In most cases they will not, because they see that you are psychologically prepared for the "attack." You have shown that you are not available as an easy victim.

That is an unpleasant experience for them, too, as they see that they have misjudged the situation. That may even deter them from attempting to abuse you again.

The survival instinct is most fully actualized in women as the maternal instinct.

Let's look at a case that we often see at RMCAT and which is consistent with anecdotal evidence on this subject.

A woman in the class may have been forcibly raped at some point in time, and she is now taking the course for this reason. Being raped can be extremely damaging to one's personal sense of self-worth and self-image. But that damage can be healed given time, proper counseling, and strong will. Frankly, the course has helped achieve this for a good number of these women over the years.

Let's suppose the woman being held down on the mat by the RMCAT armored assailant on top of her is indeed a rape victim. The armored instructor (assailant) may be telling her quite graphically all the ways he intends to sexually assault her.

She may have been given the strategy of momentary compliance until her assailant is comfortable and off-guard and in a compromising position before she attacks with 110% of everything she's got.

Remember in *The Wizard of OZ* that the Wicked Witch of the West said, "You have to be careful about these things or you will hurt the spell." So we are *careful at RMCAT,* but the realism of this scenario may paralyze some individuals. The scenario elicits PTSD behavior, and freezing up is one of the main ones in rape cases. The scenario can become totally real to the woman's frog brain.

Some women later ask how we knew *exactly* what her attacker said to her during the actual horrific rape. The answer is that we did not know. The armored assailant did not say those exact words. She simply heard them. This is a PTSD syndrome.

Our responsibility is to help this woman discover her inner survival instinct. If I know from her application that she has a young child, I may say "baby shoes" so that the instructor out there on the mat hears me. Most often these professionals do not even need my cue, though.

The assailant on top of her then breaths hard and says something like, "And I saw those little baby shoes out there on the porch, and when I'm done with you I'm going to find her and then the party really gets going, bitch!"

The formerly passive or "frozen" woman explodes in a mad fury like the mythical Banchi from the very depths of hell! She is possessed with the raw power that the adrenal rush gives her, and she has been instructed in small stages so that she can handle it and not flail but deliver effective, powerful strikes as she yells at the top of her lungs. This is a joy to see.

It also gives the woman an alternative ending to that movie that has played in her mind since the original attack—part of PTSD syndrome. This is important in her healing process.

We have received letters from psychiatrists or therapists telling us that when their patient returned from the course, for the first time (even after years of counseling and therapy) they were finally able to discuss the details of their assault.

The areas of the brain that deal with fear are located in the phylogenetically old structures of the brain, sometimes called the frog brain or reptilian brain.

This is an ancient concept in Chinese and other Asian philosophies.

The works of scientific neurobiological researchers like Dr. LeDoux and Dr. Doug Holt now support the frog brain concept as well. I find Dr. Cahill's work at the Irvine Center for the Neurological Basis of Learning and Memory especially relevant to the way adrenal versus non-adrenal memories are stored and recalled.

This part of our neural network (the frog brain) is engaged only during stressful events, and it is accompanied by the introduction of the adrenaline complex into the bloodstream. However, even recalling a traumatic memory can induce some of the physiological responses of the original event. Since this works at the frog brain level, recalling the event in the self-aware mind generally demands some sort of "trigger" at the frog brain level.

A common example that we have already looked at is someone rummaging through their attic and opening an old box that releases a fragrance. The fragrance may bring back an old but vivid romantic memory, one that they were not previously conscious that they still retained. The sense of smell is closely and directly wired into the frog brain.

Other triggers could be a sound, like a Huey helicopter passing overhead, or a song on the radio, or a photograph, or even high humidity. It all depends on what was present during the initial traumatic adrenal event. This mechanism of the brain is at the essence of the symptoms of Post Traumatic Stress Disorder (PTSD).

Dr. LeDoux explains that a trigger stimulus can elicit a neural response down two different brain pathways. One he terms the "high road," or the self-aware mind. The other is the "low road," or the reptilian Frog Brian.

The low road is the path the brain *will automatically* take in what is perceived as a survival situation, especially if it comes in the form of a surprise attack of some sort. For many years the

RMCAT training program has been based on these concepts, but only recently have we discovered that the scientific community is now quantifying it and subjecting this to the rigors of the scientific method.

The frog brain concept has been with us for centuries.

Let me point out that even centuries ago, those who experienced repeated combat made the same observation that high adrenal stress sends us into an altered and more primitive consciousness. In Musashi's *Book of Five Rings,* written over 300 years ago, he writes about the "way to victory." Musashi is often called the "Sword Saint of Japan." He killed many men with the sword, a good number in individual duels.

Imagine the adrenal stress in facing another trained samurai who is willing to die to kill you and who is holding a three-foot razor-sharp piece of steel. Now add that this is a weapon he has practiced using all his life. Musashi certainly knew something about the effects of adrenal stress on the body: loss of motor control, tunnel vision, auditory exclusion, etc. When I first read his book as a 14-year-old, it was all but incomprehensible to me. But after I had faced lethal combat myself, over time it became clear.

To me, Musashi's book is a treatise on how to train for actual combat, which means training to perform under very high adrenal stress and to allow the frog brain to work for you.

For example, Mussahi says, "Think neither of victory nor of yourself but only of cutting and killing your enemy." It was easy for me to dismiss that as only "samurai machismo" when I was much younger. But now I see what he meant by this. Phrased another way: "If you are thinking of yourself or of victory, then you will have difficulty cutting and killing your enemy." Musashi knew that thinking of "yourself and victory" is a super-conscious, self-aware thought and not part of the frog brain, which wields the sword in combat. If you were thinking these self-aware thoughts, you could not be in the proper mindset—the reptilian brain of autonomic response that is needed for success in combat.

But we are not samurai living in feudal Japan, but we deal with constant background stress.

We do not live in feudal Japan where we might have used that razor-sharp katana to save our lives. We do not live in the Wild West of the 1800s, either, where we would be carrying a pistol on our hip and with which we might occasionally practice since a potential enemy would be similarly armed.

But our minds work the same way under stress in our modern 21st Century. We are now constantly dealing with at least a basic background level of stress, which may be unprecedented in human history. This is partly because of the increasing speed of modern life, our less than fully functional socialization, and our evolutionary coping mechanisms, which do not prepare us well for the conflicts and stresses of today's world.

Just a bit more than a century and a half ago, time zones did not exist. Nothing happened that fast. Nothing moved faster than the fastest man on the fastest horse. It was only when the railroads came that time zones became necessary. They were agreed on and instituted by the railroad companies. Today, though, how many of us "punch the clock" when we go to work? In some workplaces, every minute recorded on that card counts.

If we do not learn to manage and reduce stress, it can kill us.

We still use the adrenal response to a threat just as it was used through its evolution, but now the nature of the threat has changed. We no longer need to escape the lion or saber-tooth tiger. Yet we still respond to the pressures of our daily modern life with some level of that same adrenal response.

By the way, if you believe in Creationism by a God, that's fine, too. Just consider that evolution may have been the process that God made to create us and the rest of this world and universe. Studies have long shown that people of strong religious faith deal with adversity better than those without such faith.

Personally, I think mankind is still sort of a "work in progress."

Earlier we compared the evolutionary "artifact" of storing fat for a famine that never comes to the adrenal response that intermittently but chronically engages in us on some level almost every day in our modern life. In short, we are preparing our bodies for a physical fight or flight that rarely comes.

Though nervous eating habits are a common result of stress, the result of habitual, even low-level adrenalization goes beyond our simply gaining weight. The main result is that our hearts give out pre-maturely. Heart attacks kill more of us than any other cause including car accidents and cancer. Disabling strokes fit into that picture, too. If we do not learn to control stress, this habitual "pumping ourselves up" for the fight that never comes may wear out our heart and circulatory system prematurely.

Even if we are not the ones slated to be taken "before our time" by a heart attack, we must train ourselves *not* to internalize the melee of conflict around us. To free ourselves from irrational fear unburdens us. This is not only about programming ourselves with rational self-dialogue for a healthier and more productive way of interpreting stress. It is to let go of "excess baggage." This means letting go of negative and painful past events that do not serve us. It means letting go of old ways of thinking about the world and especially about ourselves.

CHAPTER REVIEW

We store adrenal events in memory quite differently than we store non-adrenal events. Adrenal memories are much more vivid and persistent. They can automatically be triggered by a cue that was present during the original event. Post Traumatic Stress Disorder is a classic example of this. But we all commonly deal with low- or moderate-level adrenal events. This is why, for example, when a mid-level manager verbally attacks us at the office, we tend to internalize these memories into persistent, defeating self-dialogues. We should write down our adrenal-inducing events—those that make us angry or fearful or that make us "choke up"—and evaluate them later in our super-conscious minds to construct a new, productive self-dialogue and an understanding of the event and its "triggers."

Even motor responses to given cues learned under adrenal stress can become automatic, like stomping on the non-existent brake pedal on the passenger side of the car. Likewise, our responses to verbal attacks (or what we perceive as verbal attacks) can be "automatic" too, since we have formed responses under adrenal stress from previous events. The adrenal mind is most often separated from the rational, self-aware mind. Hence, we need to recognize our knee-jerk responses to anticipated stress and replace them with more reasoned ones.

An excessive need for the approval of others indicates an unstable, unsure self-image. We cannot base our self-worth on what we perceive that others may say or think about us. It is natural to want to be accepted, but we must not predicate our self-worth on the approval of others. We must establish an authentic personal self-worth by the strength and integrity of our own character. In this way, each day as our behavior follows congruently with that positive self-image, we reinforce and validate its unconditional reality.

We can associate three broad personality types with an excessive need for acceptance and approval:
  a) perfectionists
  b) people pleasers and
  c) enablers.

It is useful to be able to recognize these personality types. The easiest and most productive people to deal with are usually the ones with the strongest and most authentic positive self-images. This is because they are rarely afraid of losing or of losing control.

We need to be conscious of the mental traps of a) maintaining rigid rules that everyone else must follow and, b) irrational, amplified self-dialogues. These self-dialogues result from generalizing from the specific to the universal, i.e. "Judy does not want me, so I must not be worthy of any woman and will never find a mate." If we believe we will fail, we usually *will* fail. We rarely win until we feel and think and act like winners.

Socialization estranges us from some of our productive survival instincts. The predator counts on finding a passive victim of excessive socialization. The predator has a big mental advantage here due to his experience with how people react to stand-up aggression. He knows that suitable victims react with fear, denial and even paralysis. We need to acquaint ourselves with the tremendous inner power of our survival instincts before we need to summon it in crisis—be it a physical or mental crisis. Little else raises our self-worth and self-esteem as getting in touch with this inner survival instinct and its power. It makes us whole.

Adrenaline puts our bodies into "overdrive." Our heart and respiration rates increase. It dramatically enhances our tolerance to pain and our physical strength. But if we are estranged from our survival instincts through socialization and/or a lack of experience with adrenaline and real fear, then the adrenal rush can overpower us. This reality is underscored by the fact that many good martial artists are helpless in an actual fight with even a totally untrained assailant. Their martial training has been conducted in their self-aware or non-adrenal mind. Under the adrenal stress of an actual attack, they may have no access to the frog brain. The self-aware mind and the frog brain are mostly separate.

The areas of the brain that control our actions under high adrenal stress are the old structures of the brain—the frog brain. This portion responds to stimuli automatically. Hence, our response under adrenaline is pre-conditioned. This is why people may act irrationally when terrified. It is also why adrenal stress conditioning through scenario-based training is so effective as a physical self-defense method. But such training also puts one in touch with the survival self, and that benefits every aspect of their lives since it enhances the core of their being: their self-esteem and self-image. The survival instinct is most dramatically displayed in women as the protective maternal instinct. There really is no "killer instinct" in a normally balanced mind. There is only survival instinct.

If we do not learn to recognize, control and manage stress, it will significantly affect our health and the quality and length of our lives. Stress from our occupations and other stress-inducing environments can actually kill through cardiac failure. Stress kills more people in this country than do bullets and car accidents. It can happen to you, too, before you even realize the level of stress you are under or what it is doing to your mind and body.

In the next chapter we take a brief but important look at the physiological mechanisms of stress and its effect on the heart and circulatory system. You need to be able to measure your own stress load and its source before you can begin to reduce it and better manage it.

The Power of Mind Over Health

Our minds have a greater control over our health than we might realize. Recently, I asked my cardiologist why one soldier who sustains a superficial wound keeps on moving while another soldier inflicted with the same wound goes into shock and dies. I can absolutely assure you that this happens in combat.

My doctor said there was no medical reason he could think of for this given, the same non-life-threatening wound and the same blood loss. I replied that I thought the soldier died because he thought he was going to die. The doctor added that when patients come into the hospital and they say they are going to die in a few days, then most often they do.

In my work I deal with a small community of correctional officers or COs (prison guards), police officers and other law enforcement persons. These people live very stressful lives. They most often have shorter lives, they are more prone to substance abuse, and they have a high divorce rate. These are all reflections of the stress their jobs place on them.

Imagine being a guard in a maximum-security prison! It would be like being an unarmed cop in a community where everyone was a dangerous criminal and many were already proven violent killers. Please remember, the life span of prison guards, on a national basis, is much lower than the national average.

My cardiologist suggested that this was partly because the prison guards and police officers that he knew lived unhealthy life styles, were overweight, had poor diets, and drank too much.

But even so, I see poor eating and exercise habits and alcohol abuse of some COs as symptoms—self-destructive reactions to the extreme and chronic stress of their jobs. Police in general have a higher divorce rate, substance abuse rate and suicide rate than the general population. This is understandable though, isn't it?

Corrections officers have an average life expectancy of just 57 years. Consider this letter from a prison guard I know named Jim:

"I've been a CO for over 13 years. Job stress has affected me negatively, to put it mildly. My daily working environment is hostile. Much of the stress comes from managers, many of whom torment officers with petty issues in a non-ceasing deluge of harassment. They write us up for being a minute late for roll call or for not wearing a tie. Or because we called out sick. They make an issue out of small matters that force us to expend time and energy on silly issues that are a waste of time."

Whether we manage our own self-dialogues rationally or irrationally and whether we enter the reactive mind or the non-reactive mind under stress affect our physical and mental health. Chronic or "incident" depression can even lower the body's immune system. These are real.

Consider an actual case that I know of personally: A woman placed her aging mother in a nursing home. The daughter understood that her insurance would pay most of the costs. She then received a letter from the insurance company telling her that she must pay a substantial cost of her mother's care.

The cost was nearly beyond her means, and she became worried and depressed. In a little more than a day, she became sick and ran a fever. Stress had reduced the strength of her immune system and she got some "bug" that she may have otherwise avoided. Later her insurance company acknowledged that the payments were not her responsibility after all, and she recovered quickly.

Stress can be chronic or the result of an "incident." Our bodies and minds respond differently to those two types of stress.

Incident stress

What I refer to as "incident" stress is the type we observe in our adrenal stress conditioning classes at RMCAT or the type stress that a soldier feels in combat or a mother feels in rescuing her child from a vicious dog attack. Incident stress is the type most likely to affect the PTSD reaction, too.

Incident stress is the fight or flight response to danger or even the perception of danger. The heart rate increases and blood pressure rises. Blood is withdrawn from the skin (except the facial areas) and the digestive system and pumped to the muscles for a fight. Medical studies show us that our biochemical reactions to the adrenal complex release can even make our blood clot faster in case of injury.

We are thus ready to do battle with that "Neanderthal man" or to join in with the hunting party in the very dangerous task of taking down that "Woolly Mammoth" with our stone-tipped spear. This adrenal complex in our blood also gives us greatly increased physical strength and speed and tolerance to pain in order to accomplish these tasks—but at what cost?

In the somewhat ancient Chinese cosmology of life, there is a concept called "chi." It refers to inner strength and the "essence of the thing" or life energy and focus of internal strength.

It is through their mastery of their chi that Taoist and other Asian monks, for example, perform what are apparently superhuman feats: breaking rocks with blows from their hands and having spear points pressed into their throats without the steel points breaking the skin.

I have seen all of these and much more in my 30-plus years of martial arts study, but I do not see anything mystical or supernatural about them. Remarkable as these feats may be, Newtonian mechanics and Western physics and human physiology are sufficient to explain them to me.

But I do find that the hypothetical concept of chi or life force has value in explaining how adrenal stress and chronic stress can negatively affect the body. One can look at one's chi as being the finite reserve of one's life energy. Hence, when we go into the adrenal state over a fight or flight incident, we are throwing more of our finite life's energy onto the metabolic furnace or our "fire of life." We are stomping our foot on the gas pedal of our car and burning up our limited fuel supply to get somewhere or away from something fast!

But when we burn up our fuel reserves this fast to accomplish that fight or flight task, we also put extra strain and wear on our "engines." The engine of our body is our heart. It has to beat constantly; when it stops, then so will we. Adrenaline makes our blood clot faster if we are injured in fight. But that same adrenaline may also allow a piece of plaque to dislodge from the interior of an artery and cause a heart attack.

Chronic stress

In chronic stress, we are constantly in a state of elevated awareness for a danger that has not yet manifested. An extreme example would be a soldier clearing a minefield. He sweeps his magnetometer (mine detector) over the ground, extremely vigilant to the telltale pinging sound of metallic mine detection.

He can't afford to miss even one mine. He can't afford a single mistake: He is dead or his legs are blown off or some trooper later might suffer that same fate.

The mine clearer pays a price for enduring this high level of stress, this accelerated burning of his life's energy. Fortunately, he is generally a younger man and has more life energy to expend.

The brain and the body work together to identify the proper response to a particular adrenal eliciting situation. Is this a true fight or flight incident where danger is right here and now? Or is the adrenal release a demand for a higher state of alertness for a danger that may suddenly present itself?

Chronic stress seems to be more destructive to the heart and circulatory system than is incident stress. Consider the shorter life spans of police officers and especially prison guards (COs). Convicts do not attack the prison guards that often, really. But the prison guard must always be totally vigilant for the cues of an attack to maximize their chances to survive. This is the essence of chronic stress: extreme and constant vigilance.

Chronic stress in the office

An office worker such as a secretary who is constantly "putting out fires" in the office and who seems to be responsible by default for anything that no one else is responsible for, likely feels that their life is *out of control.*

The chronic stress of their workplace has pre-empted and distorted their lives. They begin to experience their job as being their life, and they can't leave it at the office when they get home. It permeates all aspects of their lives. It can actually poison their lives in a very important sense.

One might think that those with the highest levels of responsibility such as key executives or CEOs might have the greatest stress levels. Perhaps some do, but apparently these CEO types handle stress better than the secretary we mentioned. Why?

It is partly because the person with the greater responsibility is the upper-level manager. He has more power and control over his working environment than does the lower-level employee like the secretary. Again, we see that the feeling of not being in control is at the root of fear and anxiety. We might also speculate that those who become upper-level mangers have a stronger and more confident self-image. Thus they naturally handle stress better.

Perhaps the more damaging and most common stress is that which results in a person feeling no control over their work environment. If they identify their lives as their work, then they feel that they have lost control over their lives, too.

Again, let's listen to the voice of a man who has been there and lived it—a corrections officer in a large state prison:

"One incident, in particular, was the deciding factor in my decision to go on medication. A coworker of mine went on a murder/suicide rampage. That was it. This incident drove home just how serious stress can be. Of course, I wasn't nearly to the point of picking up a firearm and killing with it, but it made an impression on me, nonetheless. I felt hopeless from being in a constant state of anxiety and panic attacks, and I felt I just had to do something. So medication it was."

How stress damages the heart and circulatory system

In recent years we have had new thinking about this question, so I will confine myself to what is now generally accepted in the medical literature.

First, when I use the term adrenaline I am collectively referring to the adrenaline complex. This includes adrenaline, cortisol, nor-adrenaline and other bio-chemicals that these release. The major damage to the heart and circulatory system, especially the blood supply to the heart, comes from this adrenal complex, which causes higher blood pressure. High blood pressure can damage the arteries and wash out chunks of arterial plaque that then can cause blood clots and a heart attack.

Before that occurs, though, the adrenaline complex ratcheting up the heart rate and blood pressure can damage the interior of the artery, creating a small pocket where blood fats collect. This in time can reduce the blood supply to the heart. In the worst-case scenario, the plaque builds up until it partially or fully closes the artery or breaks off and passes down the bloodstream to lodge in a smaller vessel and cause a blood occlusion there.

Either can result in a fatal heart attack or a disabling stroke. This is one reason why our diets can contribute to a heart attack. If we eat a lot of fat, then we have more fat in our bloodstreams to build up in these adrenaline-damaged arteries. The repeated release of the adrenal complexes from chronic stress may well be the central reason for hardening of the arteries. Genetics also plays a key factor.

The extreme case often best illuminates an operative principle. Study the prison guard's message and try to absorb what it might be like to be under this level of chronic adrenal stress:

Many times, I've said to myself and other people, 'I should not be alive today because of some of the crazy shit I did shortly after starting working at the prison.' Peyton, I did some stuff that was insane. Understand, I didn't do anything wrong. On the contrary, I did my job to the letter, which was not at all popular back then. You see, most were just trying to get by with as little trouble as possible, and here I was, trying to make a difference, doing things the right way.

All of this made me stand out. Some call it 'super-cop syndrome.' I realize now that I was a fucking idiot. I did no good, received no reward. In fact, all I did was hurt myself. Luckily, despite being in several deadly situations, I didn't get seriously hurt, nor get anyone else hurt.

So yes, I look back these days and think, damn, I can't believe I took all those chances like that. When I think back, I thank God that I got through it physically okay. Mentally, I was another story. PTSD, anxiety, depression, all plagued me to the point that I was nearly non-functional.

Taking a vacation is a mixed blessing. This year, I took a week off. As I drove down the road away from the prison, about to begin my vacation, I was actually high. Not from drugs, alcohol, or any foreign substance. Rather, I was high because I knew I didn't have to go into that place for an entire week. I was physically shaking!

But even when a vacation is upon me, when it's just beginning, I know that I'll have to go back. It's not so bad these days, but a few years ago, it was difficult to return to the prison after a vacation. Or even just after taking my regular days off! There were times when I wanted to call in sick, but knew that I shouldn't, just because I was experiencing such dread and anxiety at the thought of returning to the prison. Many times, I was in tears because of it.

Taking a week or two off reminds me of what it's like to be a normal person. After a few days, I realize that there are people who don't have to look over their shoulder because people want to kill them. They don't have to keep their guard up all the time because someone might stab them in the kidneys. I want to be one of the ignorant people who doesn't have to do all of that.

I'm handling it much better, though, these days. I think it's because the prison isn't as violent as it used to be, though that could change quickly. I don't have as much dread these days. I realize that it's a job that has to be done.

Still, there are times when I think about the worst. What would become of my family if I'm killed? Will my kids be okay? Who will help raise them? Will they turn out okay?

In years past, I felt as if I were on one of those World War II bombers in which the crew never knew if it would be their last mission. The mission in which everyone "gets it," gets killed. That's what each day was like for me when the prison was at it's most violent. Every day was a mission in which we were uncertain if we'd survive. I imagine that's what war is like. But in war, your time there is finite; if you're not killed, you get rotated home after usually a year or so. With COs, we have to do a career.

This man knows the level of stress he is dealing with. But it is clear that many people do not consciously realize the level of stress that their jobs, relationships or other life circumstances place on them, because stress can distort their thinking and rationality. That is until they escape the stress and look back on the situation. Then they might say to themselves, "What the hell was I thinking to work at that job! I must have been crazy."

We do not always recognize the level of stress we are under—even high levels of stress.

This is paradoxical: When subjected to continual, daily amounts of great stress, the mind may sublimate it. We do not realize the pressure we are under until it is relieved and we leave the stressful environment.

Some of the wartime PTSD experiences operate in this manner too. In the combat zone the soldier can't afford to fully engage everything that is happening, or he will be overcome by it and distracted from staying alive and supporting the fire team. But when he gets home and the stress is relieved, it may all hit him hard and vividly.

More than a few prison guards have told me that they are OK on the job. They will even casually e-mail me about today's fatal stabbing or the suicide of an inmate as if they were making small talk.

But when they go on vacation, as we have read, they suffer terrible anxiety at the thought of *returning to* the prison. Again, they become aware of the amount of stress they were carrying only *when it is removed.*

A personal experience with stress

At one point in my life, I wanted a simple cash business that required only two or three employees, so I got into the liquor store business.

I had several armed robberies, and I always carried a pistol in a shoulder holster or kept one under the counter. I have been around firearms since I was a pre-teenager, so I am comfortable, well trained, and familiar with firearms, from pistols to belt-fed machine guns. Still, I never forget the deadly or life-crippling potential of firearms if handled irresponsibly.

I am a fast and accurate shooter. Before going in to open my liquor store, I would draw my weapon several times to make sure it would not hang up on my clothing. But I know from experience that pistol-caliber bullets do not often immediately stop an animal as large as a human. The idea of the faster draw meaning the difference between life and death in the old west gunfight is almost pure mythology. If one man were a fraction of a second or even a full second faster than the other was, it most likely just would not matter. Shooting the other man would not likely stop him from firing his own weapon. Consequently, both men may well kill each other regardless of who was faster on the draw.

It just isn't like in the movies where people are shot with a little twenty-five auto, and then they drop dead immediately. Unless the bullet enters the brain case, ruptures the left ventricle of the heart, or severs the spinal cord, there is no medical reason why the person hit by a pistol-caliber bullet cannot return fire. I was quite aware of this when I ran my liquor store.

What I was *not* aware of was the great stress that running the place and the armed robberies was putting on me. All of this was on top of having to deal with the general public every day.

To make it short, the great state of Colorado, in its infinite wisdom, decided to remove and rebuild the bridge that allowed traffic to come my store. The construction put an end to my business just like twisting a water faucet. People could not get to my store.

I labored to salvage the operation, but ultimately I knew it was not achievable. I let the state have the place for back taxes at a significant financial loss.

Yet, after about a week of not strapping on that pistol before opening the store, I realized what tremendous stress I had been under. It felt like a great weight had been removed. My financial loss almost paled compared to the new sense of freedom and escape that I felt. I had turned the loss into a positive.

In leaving the old business, it was now possible to move on to something better.

Examine the incident and chronic stress you might be under.

Examine your life, occupation, and perhaps even your personal relationships and try to measure the level of both incident and especially chronic stress that they place you under.

If you hate your job and feel nothing but contempt for your managers, then you are in an unhealthy situation. You may have to decide which is more important—*you* or that job? Because those really are the stakes involved. I cannot imagine choosing a job over my own physical and mental well-being.

I live in the real world the same as you, my friend. I know that we all must make a living and support those dependent on us, and this is seldom easy for anyone. But weigh this into the balance: That job you hate may be slowly wrecking your physical and mental health, but think even further than that. What is it doing to your family? Are you irritable? Do you have occasional fits of rage at home? When you get home from work on Friday nights, do you plop down into that easy chair and reach for a six-pack of beer or some whiskey and turn on the TV?

If so, then your job just may not be worth what you are paying in the quality and length of your life. Do not let fear make you think that you have no choice. That is the mentality of the victim. That kind of thinking never serves you. If you allow yourself to believe that you have no way out, then you are right. But the *converse* is also true. This is the same old "self-fulfilling prophecy" mental trap at work.

There are always options in these situations. But you need the courage to engage them. In the case of the disabling job, it is mostly a matter of letting go. That can be hard, of course, until you allow yourself to see the total picture with clarity. Once you clearly and correctly define your goals, then your choices are much easier.

Perhaps you have heard the Zen parable of the man who fell into a fast-running river. The man encountered a large rock as he went downstream, and he clung to that rock for his life.

As he desperately held onto the rock against the powerful current, his body was beaten and bloodied against the rock. A monk on shore seeing this yelled, "Let go of the rock! Let go and flow downstream or you will be beaten to death by the current."

Do you need to let go of the rock?

There were times in my life when I did, but it took banging and bloodshed for me to see that. The liquor store was a prime example.

Dealing with the biggest fear of all: aging and death

Your time on this planet is finite and will expire like a parking meter at some point in the future. None of us knows when that will occur—not with absolute certainty anyway. It is only rational to make important life decisions taking this important and inescapable reality into account.

Some people are dying to retire; don't be one of them.

Your occupation is not your life, or at least you should not allow it to be.

Your choice of a job or career is a major life decision. It is a statistical reality that a disproportionate number of people who retire at say age 65 die several months or just a few years later. They made their job their life, so when their job was done, so were they. This can be true even if they despised their job—perhaps especially true if they despised their job.

In making a decision as important as leaving a job that is destroying or pre-empting your life, it is relevant to consider the statistics of how much time you have remaining to live. Also consider the quality of your life in your twilight years. Consider the health problems you may have when you move into your mid-fifties. Some of the things you may enjoy now—active sports, surfing, riding a motorcycle, sex, sailing or whatever—may not be as possible for you to enjoy in your later years.

This is not too difficult to imagine, is it? Remember what sex was like when you were 18 years old? I am 53 years old and I can recall the difference, though I still have sexual relations with my wife. I can also remember when I could fight in judo tournaments and defeat one opponent after another though each new opponent was fresh and I had just fought the last one.

Well, now those days are gone and like the song says, "Those days are gone forever and I should just let them go." I just am glad I made the best of them, that I drank fully the wine of my youth while I could.

Our later years—55 and older—can be happy and fulfilling if we make them so. But we had better start preparing to make them that way now by enjoying life and letting go of our irrational fears and reactive mind.

"Going postal"

It is not the length of life but the quality of life that is more important. We build the foundation for financial security, if there is to be such a thing, mostly when we are younger. But is it worth trading the 40 years between ages 25 and 65 working in a large, high volume and high-pressure "post office," just waiting for that retirement pension? Only you can make that decision. It may indeed be the correct decision for you.

Today we have a cultural characterization termed "going postal." Now think about why that term was formed. I think many of the people who enter postal work tend to be more security oriented. They are driven more by a fear of loss and by insecurity than by the hope of achieving something better in their lives. The pressure of their postal careers eats away at some of them year after year.

One day, perhaps over some incident-type job stress, their accumulation of chronic stress causes *cascade failure*. But let's be fair here—this extreme happens only to a very, very small minority of postal workers. At the same time let's not forget the report of that homicidal /suicidal prison guard's bloody rampage.

The ones who do go down this path may wake up one day and realize that they are past middle age and that they have never really "lived" yet. But they will not accept responsibility for their situation. They do not see it as the result of the many choices they made for themselves much earlier on.

Instead, they often direct responsibility for their misery, helplessness, powerlessness and hopelessness toward others. Often this will be their managers or co-workers.

They feel that their lives are out of control, and they feel frustrated and powerless. That feeling is intolerable, and they rage against it. They are driven to show that they do have control and power and that they do "count." They need to show everyone at their workplace (and perhaps beyond) that they cannot be abused with impunity. They demonstrate that there will now be a high price to pay for it.

In some tragic cases this means that they come to work one day with a gun and shoot several people to death before they take their own lives or commit "suicide by police."

How much stress are you under? It can be measured.

Blood pressure is a well-accepted measure of stress. Blood pressure is a measure of force or pressure the heart employs to pump blood through our bodies. There are two readings: one when the heart is pumping and one when it is at rest (receiving new blood) between beats. These are called the systolic pressure (the maximum pressure in the artery when the heart is pumping) and the diastolic pressure (the lower pressure between beats).

Blood pressure is recorded as the systolic pressure over the diastolic pressure. For example, a blood pressure reading might be 120 over 80. This would be a "normal" reading.

A person with high blood pressure might have a reading of 140/90. Most physicians consider anything higher than this to be dangerous. Low blood pressure, on the other hand, is generally not a problem if it is not caused by some pathology or trauma (i.e., a bleeding wound of some sort). People who are young and healthy, such as physically fit teenagers, can have blood pressure readings as low as 97/55.

Your blood pressure is a fairly good measure of the overall health of your total cardiovascular system. Normal levels of blood pressure mean the heart is working normally. High levels of blood pressure mean the heart is working extra hard just to keep the blood pumping. If the heart has to work extra hard to keep blood flowing, such as in obese persons, then it can become enlarged. An enlarged heart is very serious high risk sign of a heart attack.

In simple terms, the harder the heart has to work, the faster it is going to wear out. High blood pressure signals possible damage to the arteries. This arterial damage can allow blood fats to be deposited in the artery. This constricts the artery, reducing blood flow.

If the artery becomes completely or nearly closed by this arterial plaque or if a portion of this plaque is dislodged by the flow of the blood's elevated pressure, then that plaque can flow down the bloodstream to occlude a smaller arterial passage. In either case, we have a heart attack or a stroke.

Fortunately, now small and relatively inexpensive blood pressure meters ($50 to $85) are available. They are computerized and strap onto the wrist so you can measure your own blood pressure as frequently as you wish. These devices must be used properly to get a correct reading. It is advisable to compare your instrument's reading to the reading you are given in your physician's office.

In many cases high blood pressure can be effectively treated with existing and well-proven drugs. It is also easy to diagnose. Yet high blood pressure often goes undiagnosed for many years. Medical studies suggest that as many a 25% or more of Americans have high blood pressure. But as many as one third of these people do not even know that they have this condition! High blood pressure can result in a fatal heart attack or disabling stroke. This can be prevented in many cases if people will have their blood pressure examined by a physician and then follow a program of diet and exercise.

I feel that a significant amount of high blood pressure is due to the stress in our modern lives, much of which, like high blood pressure itself, we remain unaware of. But a genetic factor is involved here too. If your family is prone to high blood pressure or heart attacks, then that is all the more reason to see a physician. You need to understand the root causes of your stress and how to manage it better.

We can affect some control over the reduction of that arterial and cardiac damage and our blood pressure levels by organizing and changing our thought patterns in response to stress. Changing our internal self-dialogues is one way to do that. Of course diet and exercise are another essential tool to reduce stress and the potential for heart failure. Today's new drugs can help many people avoid a heart attack too.

However, you had better see your doctor before you have that first heart attack, as there is no drug that can raise the dead.

Do not underestimate the impact your mental state has on your heart and general health. The way you think can have a significant and even decisive impact on both. Remember the two soldiers with nearly identical superficial wounds? One lived because he though he would live, and the other died because he thought he would die. We might also say he died because he feared he would die. Recall my own cardiologist who said that people who came into the hospital saying that they were going to die in few days very often did just that.

Some people are brain-wired for a high adrenal response to stress.

I am certain that you have dealt with people who sometimes "fly off the handle" over what seems like a trivial thing. If you think about these cases, you might see that the trivial incident was not really what caused the over-reaction or "amplification" of the event (like not having the right mustard for the burgers).

The real cause was what came before. The incident was just the final straw that broke the dammed-up reservoir of chronic stress that they were accumulating daily. I submit that if they had recognized the damage that the stress was doing to them both mentally and physically, and if they had developed a positive self-image, then they would have been strongly motivated to modify their stressful environment and the way they processed that stress.

You *must* be strongly motivated to change your stress levels by the way you mentally interpret stressful situations. I know it is possible to do so, and since it is your very life that may be on the line here, I hope you can generate that motivation. You need a strong sense of personal self-worth to accomplish that. You need to know that you are worth fighting for and that your job is not worth dying for.

The best and perhaps the only way to overcome fear is to face it.

In our RMCAT training we put people under high adrenal stress for short periods so that they can learn to manage that stress. Teaching self-defense without adrenal stress is like teaching people to swim without water.

Years ago I realized that people came to these classes to learn to de-escalate confrontations and sometimes to conquer a particular fear. Sometimes it was to overcome anxiety and damage to their self-esteem over a violent incident. They came as much to achieve personal self-improvement as to learn effective self-defense.

These people leave with an enhanced and clarified sense of self-worth and self-competence. This is because they have done something. They have not just sat in a chair and been entertained by a charismatic lecturer. They have *taken a risk and directly faced their fear.* They have learned to manage that fear and even turn it into something productive.

They also discover that they are not alone in their fears. They all get the total support of the entire class in achieving their goals, and that is very important to the process. We are social animals.

However, since we are dealing with adrenalizing people at RMCAT, it is prudent to check their blood pressure from time to time to make sure we are not going to aggravate an existing high blood pressure condition. A baseline blood pressure reading is taken a few hours after they get to the ranch training complex from the airport. Later, more readings are taken during class.

As you would expect, people's blood pressure rises significantly when they enter the scenarios with the armored

Bulletman assailant or "woofer." It even rises while they are in the line waiting for their scenario to come up!

Even when the confrontation has not yet gotten physical but is just a "hot verbal woofing" interview, the student's blood pressure will rise as will their respiration and heartbeat.

It is an open-ended scenario for them too, as a rule. For example, if the student successfully projects a very strong, congruent and fully assertive verbal boundary, the armored instructor may back off just as an actual "woofing" bully might do in real life.

The hyper responders to the adrenal rush

Blood pressure levels rise even more sharply *for most people* in the course when it goes to a physical fight. A point I want to underscore here is that for a few people, blood pressure will rise dramatically even under the hot, verbal "interview" drills. Their blood pressure sometimes won't go any higher even when the fight gets physical. These people might be called "hyper responders."

We watch these people carefully and give them special attention, measuring their responses and blood pressure closely. With each new scenario, the student gains better control of their vocal centers, their visual processing and their motor control. As I said previously, I have seen good black belts flail like children in the first few adrenal stress-driven fight scenarios. This is mystifying to them when they see it on videotape, but my staff almost expects it.

However, as they get further exposure to the scenario, we see greater motor control and even slightly lower blood pressure readings. Their bodies are learning to control and manage the adrenal flow. They are accomplishing this in the best, and perhaps the only way possible, which is by actually experiencing it.

Even the hyper responders make progress here, but not as well as the normal responders in terms of blood pressure spike reduction.

You should investigate if you are a hyper responder. In the doctor's office, it is natural to be a little nervous and to show a slightly higher blood pressure reading than normal. What I call a hyper responder could be missed by just a blood pressure test alone. We need to see how their blood pressure responds under adrenal stress.

An experiment to identify hyper responders

As an experiment, in some classes I had the attendants play the computer video game Tomb Raider. The idea was to see if I could identify hyper responders by measuring their blood pressure as they played the game. The problem with this experimental design was a confounding of variables and a non-normalized sample space.

Some people had played video games before and were used to them. Others had played this particular video game dozens and dozens of times already, and others had no interest in them and had never played any video game. Frankly, I do not have much interest in video games either.

The only thing we could see for sure was that people's blood pressure tended to go up when they played the games. In fact, there was evidence that it went up highest in people who were familiar with the game and liked playing it and who were good at it. Could this possibly be due to the endorphins released in what has come to be called "runner's high"?

Or, perhaps it was because they were competing with themselves to get a higher score with the game. Maybe they were just hooked on playing that particular game. The experimental design did not allow us the data to know.

Since we seem to be able to identify the hyper responder when we measure their blood pressure under stress, and that may not happen in doctor's office, it is helpful to recognize behaviors that are associated with people who overreact to adrenal situations.

I will make a final note on people's responses to the stress of the scenarios. Most everyone reports that the most difficult and stressful part of the scenarios is the time between the Bulletman assailant first coming out and starting to talk, woof, or interview them, and the time the physical fight starts.

In other words, the lead up to the fight was more stressful for them than the physical fight itself. This is because they are in their self-aware, super conscious minds when being "woofed on" and "interviewed." That self-aware part of the brain is the level of consciousness that interprets and analyses. But it is not specifically or exclusively set up to deal with flight or fight situations.

Once they get into the physical portion of the fight, they go into their non-self-aware adrenal mind (frog brains), which is set up for the fight or flight response but which is not so self-aware. The adrenal mind does not engage or reflect or make analytical decisions. It acts out of survival instinct. This is why the attendants report that they are more stressed and scared by the interview than by the actual fight.

Perhaps you have heard people say after a near-fatal encounter, "Everything happened too fast for me to be afraid." What really occurred was that they went into their frog brain automatically. The frog brain acts, and it does not feel fear in the conventional, self-aware sense.

It is uncertainty itself that we often fear the most. So, we must get accustomed to living with uncertainty, because nothing is really certain except change itself.

It is also the feeling of not being in control that causes significant stress. But we can't always control our environment. This is why we must always try to control our own mind and our own rational thinking. If we can do this, we can control our fear.

Wasn't the act of driving a little scary when you first got your driver's license?

Here are a few examples that identify the hyper responder and may shed light on the phenomena of "road rage." But first let's consider how your attitude toward driving a car, which always has an element of danger, has changed through experience.

Driving in traffic can be stressful. But think back to how much more stressful it was the first few days after you got your driver's license. Driving was new to you and an unknown danger. But now it isn't, is it?

The danger of driving is no different now than back then. In fact, the danger may even be greater now than years ago when you got your license. This may be due to increased traffic and perhaps more mentally unstable drivers on the road. But your attitude about driving and your initial fear of doing something wrong has changed with the familiarity of driving.

This demonstrates that you can change the way you mentally interpret stressful events. Take a moment to imagine how much your attitude toward driving has changed since the stress you experienced as a beginning driver. If you can learn to drive a car safely and competently and yet carry on a pleasant conversation with your passenger, then you can change the way you interpret stressful events.

Yet somewhere in your mind you still know that every time you get behind that wheel, you are taking your life into your hands, and the lives of others as well. You just don't let this bother you, as you are confident of your driving skills. You know you can handle it. This is the attitude we need to develop regardless of what the stressful situation may be.

Road Rage: This is often a sign of a hyper responder. Inside the confines of their steel cage, they feel safe and empowered. But it is intolerable to them when someone pulls in front of them and forces them to slow down. Their internal and irrational self-dialogue goes something like this: "Goddamn that son of bitch! What the hell is he thinking? He thinks he can control me! He thinks he can force me to go *at his pace.* He acts like I am not even here. Does he think I'm powerless to do anything about it? Well I'll show that damn bastard who has the power! Arggh!"

Now if the driver is a hyper responder in the grip of adrenal road rage, they may do something to endanger their life and that of others. They will pass in a no-passing zone. They may get within a foot or so of the other guy's rear bumper and stay there. This is like the bully who got up to stand over me in the bar. It is a form of "postural intimidation." But like all irrational, fear-based behavior it is counter productive. In this case, it even works against our own survival.

For the road rage driver, the guy pulling out in front of him was the same as not getting his "props." "Road rage boy" saw the other driver as showing disrespect by pulling out in front of him—much like the convict who did not return the cigarette. With the horsepower and rolling steel, road rage can end in homicide too.

The road rage driver has allowed his reservoir of unresolved stress to overcome his rationality. The guy pulling out in front of him and thus "dissing him" (being disrespect to him) by not giving him the road is just the trigger that vents that great reservoir of rage. The road rage driver feels that the car empowers him and he is now going to use that power to compensate for feelings of powerlessness in his life as a whole.

Responding rationally to difficult drivers

The person who maintains a strong personal self-image and a feeling of self-competence and self-control seldom feels powerless. It is easier for them to re-process this driving experience rationally, even if they still aren't pleased with the other driver's behavior.

Their rational self-dialogue might go like this: "That imbecile! They saw me coming and they pulled out like that anyway! OK, breathe and relax. I won't be trapped into purely re-active mindset here. I am not going to let *anyone* control my actions and thoughts but me, and not that moron up there, no matter what he does. I am not going to let this sub-human trash force me into doing something stupid that might put me in prison. Something like forcing his car off the cliff up there where it would hit the rocks below and explode into a roaring ball of orange flame, as satisfying as that might be to witness."

Well OK, this colorful imagery works for me, and as I said before I believe it is healthy to have an active fantasy life and to use humor too.

But you may be more mentally stable than I, so here is an alternative self-dialogue that might fit you better: "Why did they do that? They certainly saw me coming. Were they so old they can't judge my speed or distance? Well OK, relax now. I travel this road all the time and I know there will be a safe place to pass in four miles or so. I am going take some deep abdominal breaths and let go of this incident now and feel better."

Now if you are even more rational and at peace with yourself, you might even be able to think like this: "Those people should not have pulled out in front of me like that. They don't seem to be very alert drivers, so I am going to keep some distance from them. They are going rather slow too, but even if I have to stay behind them all the way to County Road 24, it will still only delay me a few minutes at most. I guess it isn't the few minutes I may lose that bothers me. It's that I feel they disrespected me by pulling out like that and they prevented me from being in control of my own car's speed. But that is irrational thinking. They likely don't know I'm even here. They are apparently just oblivious. I won't waste any energy letting this thing upset me."

Standing in Line "Disorder": Do you sometimes feel anxiety over standing in line? Will you pass by a restaurant where were intending to eat if you see too many cars in the parking lot and there will be a line to get seated? If you are eating at a fast food place and they get your order wrong, do you explode, go back to the front of the line, and demand loudly that they get it right, and right away? Have you ever thrown your hamburger back at the people behind the counter or onto the floor because they got your order wrong? If so, then you are very likely a hyper responder to adrenal stress. We have already examined rational and irrational self-dialogues to this fast food, waiting-in-line situation.

I somewhat cured myself of this problem by simply facing it. I went to a few crowded fast food places and waited in line as I mentally recited my rational, waiting-in-line self-dialogue. I still do not like to wait in line, understand, but I know now that if I really need to, then I can handle it with a lot less stress.

Hypoglycemia

Another possibility is that you may get irritable and highly stressed because of hypoglycemia (low blood sugar attacks). In severe cases, this can affect your brain and behavior and make you more aggressive and even combative in ways that are close to being beyond your control if it is not recognized and handled properly.

I have had hypoglycemia myself on occasion. I found that by eating a high-protein breakfast in the morning, like steak or eggs and beef, I could most often avoid hypoglycemic disorders for the rest of the day. Eating cereals that have refined sugars for breakfast will aggravate hypoglycemia.

If you have hypoglycemia, the sugar in that cereal may give you a short and quick feeling of energy and satisfy your morning hunger, but it can cause you to feel very hungry and even nervous just before lunch. Dense proteins rather than sugars and carbohydrates take a longer time to digest, so they tend to stabilize blood sugar better throughout the day. The old saying, "Breakfast is the most important meal of the day" I have found to be true.

Do you feel uncomfortable around crowds?

Do you avoid crowds? Do you go to a public event and then see so many people there that you change your mind and go home even though you have already paid for your ticket? Do you sometimes not go to theaters because they are crowded? Do you ever avoid public events because you think, "God knows what germs might be in the air with all those people around!"

When I studied psychology at the university several decades ago, they had all kinds of names for these disorders. But I feel that many of these behavioral labels are primarily rooted in how one has learned to respond to the adrenal stress reaction.

The more odd or irrational the behavior (like fearing a crowd because of the germs in the air or throwing a hamburger), the more likely we are dealing with a hyper responder.

We naturally avoid what we fear. Sometimes this is rational.

We avoid the things we fear. If we avoid crowds, we need to recognize that we also *fear crowds*. Anger and fear are almost inseparable.

Often we fear things that we feel powerless to control, especially when we perceive that they may be a physical or psychological threat. So is it really illogical or irrational to fear large crowds at a sporting event or a rock concert? I would have to say that no, it is not irrational. People have been trampled to death in crowds. Further, if there are communicable diseases such as the flu going around, it may be rational to avoid being exposed to so many people at that time.

But there is the key, too: If it is a rational decision, then it is not (or at least not entirely) an irrational fear-based action. We want to identify and reduce or eliminate our *irrational fears,* the ones that needlessly limit our potentials and freedom.

However, our rational fears are another matter. They serve us well if we listen to their message in our bodies and in our minds. Remember, if there is some doubt, then there is no doubt. Listen to and "go with your gut" when dealing with a rational fear.

Recall that I have had more than a few highly ranked martial arts instructors tell me that they were hospitalized by an attack by a broken-down, homeless person at the ATM. They usually saw him before they went into the ATM, and they knew something wasn't quite right. But they dismissed this rational fear and went ahead. They failed to "go with their gut," so they paid a price.

By the way, what if these people stake a large part of their personal self-image on being a third degree black belt and well able to take care of themselves in a fight? If so, getting beaten up by a broken-down alcoholic bum is also an attack of their self-image. I think this may be one of the reasons we get some of these black belt instructors in our RMCAT classes too.

But the important thing regarding the people who come here (some are martial artists and many are not) is that they have already accepted and have not denied their problem. The black belt that was beaten up at the ATM is taking positive action to overcome the insult to their personal self-image. And for that positive action to be real, they know they have to risk something.

A woman whose personal self-image has been damaged by the abominable crime of rape comes here to help transcend her fears and to repair and enhance her feelings about herself. And for that to be real, she knows she has to risk something too.

Whose decision is it—yours, or your fear's?

People interpret the same event differently. For example, suppose it rains. The rancher thinks, "Thank God my hay field is saved!" But the skier thinks, "Damn it, we should have snow by now, not rain!" The guy who wants to ride his motorcycle that weekend says to himself, "Shit, it's raining again."

Who is right? Obviously that question is without meaning. They are all right in the way that they have emotionally processed the event.

My point is that if a psychologist tells you that you have a real problem with agoraphobia or claustrophobia because you cannot go to an amphitheater or get on a commercial plane, you might have a problem. But then again, you might not. You may have no desire to go to an amphitheater or get on a plane.

But if you feel afraid even contemplating being in a crowd or on an airplane, then the decision is not yours. It is an irrational fear-based response that may need addressing and modifying. The question you should ask yourself is, "Does this attitude serve me or does it limit me?"

If you would love to see Bruce Springsteen live in concert, but your fear of crowds keeps you away, then it is a fear-based response. You have not made a decision for yourself; your fear has made the "decision" for you.

Alternatively, if you do not like concerts because you just don't like to go to events with big crowds, then your decision may be right for you. You can slap a CD of Bruce into your CD player and crank up his music in your own home or car. It would seem silly to me for anyone—even a therapist—to insist that you overcome this "fear of crowds" by engaging in an activity that you just simply find unpleasant.

What excess baggage are you bringing to the party?

The guy who went into full road rage because a car pulled in front of him was not reacting solely to the event at hand. He had brought a reservoir of stress with him that the traffic event triggered. If he had recognized that stress was building up in his workplace or in his personal relationships, then he might have employed methods to ease the stress before he encountered this trigger. Then he could have handled traffic more rationally and safely.

Even in the old days of my bar work, it was clear to me that a fight seldom broke out because of what was said or done in the bar. The combatants had brought "excess baggage" with them—unresolved hostility over past events from the previous day or the previous decade or when they were small children.

In addition to rational and self-reinforcing self-talk, we have another tool for dissolving self-limiting and self-defeating, irrational fear-based behavior. That tool is the rational analysis of our true motivations. What directs our behavior beyond what is occurring at a given moment? Analyzing each new stressful encounter teaches us more about how our brain has been wired and about what triggers our reservoir of stress.

Once we are aware of the deeper motivations behind our irrational behavior, we can begin to change automatic responses to triggering events into self-aware responses that are rational, less fear-based and that bring us closer to our goals. But to do this we have to let go of our moments of reactive mindset. This is certainly possible. I saw and experienced that in my bar work.

As long as I felt irrational fear at a patron's threats, the fear dominated my actions and dictated my responses. Then there was often violence. But when I let go of the irrational fear while also staying in touch with my frog brain's messages, that is when I was the "jockey" riding the "racehorse" (and not the other way around). Then almost everything changed for me in that extreme environment of stress. I was often able to achieve my goal, which was to get the demanded behavior from the combative patron, and without violence.

If I can use the cognitive approach and rational self-dialogue to my benefit, then so can you. We are all unique, but we are also all fundamentally made of the same "clay." Besides, if the approach I have described for dealing with hostile people worked on those assault-prone barroom bullies, is it not reasonable that it should work for you against the verbally abusive office bully?

Our personal "worldview"

Our personal self-image is our own view of ourselves and our self-worth. Our worldview is the way we see the external world. Of course, one influences the other, to some extent. Or as Christians say, "We all see through a glass darkly." That is, our interpretation of what is happening around us is not totally objective; it is filtered and processed by our personal worldview.

Our worldview may include irrational rules or unrealizable expectations. We already have looked at some of the rigid self-rules. For example: "Everybody should always be on time, all the time." Since not everybody can be on time all the time, this is an unrealizable expectation and an irrational, rigid worldview. It programs us for amplification of our stress when we have to wait for someone who is late. Thus, this portion of a worldview does not serve us.

How does our worldview develop? Where does it come from? Like a good deal of personality, much of our worldview develops in childhood. In part, it may be copied from our parents or other guardians. If you think about it, you can probably identify some behavior, even a near ritualistic behavior, that you "inherited" from those who raised you.

For my wife, one such behavior seems to be cleaning the counter after each step in cooking. But when I cook, I expect things to fall onto the counter. When I have finished cooking, I just clean the counter once. My guess is that my beloved wife learned this worldview about clean kitchen counters from her mother. She will sometimes even step in and try to clean up after me even as I cook!

Reaction formation and cognitive dissonance

Our worldview is also the product of our individual experiences in life. This can include the negative elements of reaction formation and cognitive dissonance. For example, some parents raise and prepare their children to deal with the world *as they wish it could be* rather than how it *actually is*.

These parents maintain the irrational worldview that if they can change their children into the kind of people that they want everyone in the world to be, then they can change the world itself. This irrational worldview programs children for reaction formation and cognitive dissonance later when they enter the outside world and discover how it truly is.

Cognitive dissonance results from having two diametrically opposing models in one's conscious mind. For example, the child may be taught to be polite to everyone, so their worldview is that everyone should be polite. Yet when they interact with others, they discover that not everyone is polite all the time. Some people are deliberately mean. The child experiences cognitive dissonance; the two models they have of the world just don't match up.

From cognitive dissonance can come reaction formation. This is similar to amplification. In reaction formation, the child's irrational internal dialogue may go like this: "My parents lied to me. They did not prepare me for success with their naive view of the world. Everything else they taught me must be a lie too. I can't even trust my parents, so I can't trust anybody in this garbage can of a world!" Consider for a moment how this attitude somewhat reflects the lifestyle and thinking of some young people today who call themselves Gothics.

How your worldview can amplify a stressful situation

The first thing I try to do when I am, to be blunt about it, pissed off at someone or some situation is to see if an irrational worldview—that is, a "must be" or "everyone must do" rule of mine—has been broken.

Inflexible self-rules make up a large part of our worldview, so we should identify them in ourselves. These are self-rules such as: "Everyone should have their order ready when they get to the counter," or "People should not make irrelevant small talk with clerks when I am waiting behind them to check out," or "People should treat me with the same respect I treat others."

Once we understand that our reaction and interpretation of the situation is just as much predicated on our internal and irrational self-rule (worldview) as on the others person's behavior, then we can move to modify that rigid rule.

We might say to ourselves, "I think everyone should have their order ready when they get to the fast food counter, but that is an unrealistic expectation. So maybe I should modify my worldview to 'I would like everybody to be prepared when they get to the counter.' But it would be self-defeating for me to expect that everybody will be prepared with their order all the time. That is not a realistic expectation. I would be setting myself up for unnecessary aggravation and stress to expect or demand that they behave like that."

When worlds collide: debating religion and politics

They say we should never debate religion and politics with friends. The reason is clear: What we would be debating is our entire worldviews. When one engages a conflict involving one's entire worldview, it will be received as an attack on the other person's personal self-image. You just can't sit down with a Catholic priest and expect to give him a rational argument for atheism. His worldview makes this issue non-negotiable. If he is an effective priest, he will set up irresolvable, cognitive dissonance in you to modify your worldview. (That is, selling you on the idea that there might well be a God.) He will continue until you are motivated to partially resolve it by reaching agnostic status. From there an effective priest will then hope to bring you into the full light of God. It hardly matters if that priest is a Catholic or a Buddhist or anything else.

We must realize what the other person has at stake in any negotiation. We must recognize when our goals for another mean that they *must change their worldview.* This is not to say that changing another's worldview is impossible. Hell, to some extent that is what I am trying to do with this book.

If we do not recognize when an argument (no matter how rational or well supported it may be) *challenges a major portion of another person's world view,* then we are likely going to get a totally irrational reaction from them. We will be unable to change their worldview in the slightest way. We won't even be able to communicate with them. They simply will not hear us.

Ideally we should find a way to integrate their worldview with our argument. If a person believes God created man in His own image, it is tough to sell that person on scientific evolutionary development unless we harmonize and reconcile this concept with their belief. For example, we could suggest that evolution was God's tool to create us. In this way we do not close their minds totally to our logic. But we would have done exactly that if we *totally denied the essence of their worldview,* the belief in all-powerful, benevolent God.

Hence, we can see that a person's worldview on some subjects can make their thinking seem totally irrational to someone who does not share that worldview.

In the martial art of aikido there is a concept called blending. When the enemy attacks, we do not arrest his attack or block his attack in any conventional sense. Instead we flowingly blend with that attack. This is done so smoothly that we become one with his attack and so can redirect it harmlessly. The charging enemy may be thrown by his own redirected energy.

The aikido metaphor of blending with another's worldview to keep a dialogue open applies here. It is sometimes an element of good salesmanship too.

"I Can't" thinking

Consider a situation where a man wants his wife to go to the store for him. He is fixing the dishwasher and needs a common hardware store part. His wife says, "I can't go to the store now." But it would be more accurate for her to say, "I do not want to go to the store now."

Using the word "can't" either verbally or in our self-dialogues is often a subconscious effort to divorce ourselves from responsibility for a decision. After all, if we can't do it, then we just can't do it, so it is not our fault or our responsibility anymore.

Sometimes, of course, it is perfectly reasonable and proper for us to tell someone that we can't do something. The point here is that we need to figure out what our decisions are based on. Is a decision our own, or is it based on fear or a pre-conscious self-deception?

For example, someone who says they can't learn to drive may actually mean they are afraid to learn to drive. In conceptualizing the idea accurately, we are more in touch with the real problem and can deal with the problem better. When we stop saying "I can't do that," we begin to open up deeper communication with ourselves and with others. It is only occasionally that we actually can't do something.

Focus on what you can do rather than on what you can't.

Even when we actually can't do something, consider the conceptual difference between these two statements: "I can't possibly lift that!" as opposed to "Well Joan, if it weighed maybe 55 pounds less, then I think I could lift it." Expressing what you can do rather than what you cannot is a very good habit. This will in time reorient your thinking by changing your internal dialogue and improving your communication with others.

In telling Joan with a smile that you could lift the object if it were 55 pounds less, you communicate with her constructively. You are telling her that you would like to lift the object as she requested but that it isn't possible for you alone. Perhaps Joan will see some humor in your response, too. Humor is not only a powerful communications tool; it is also one of the best tools for getting through hard times, depression and even personal loss.

Dealing with resentment toward those that you feel have abused or betrayed you

Reaction formation often sets in against people that we feel have abused us or have betrayed our trust. This can happen with a boss or even a lover, among others. As in all reaction formation, there is the element of amplification. The boss is all bad since he did not keep his word about our promotion or did not give us credit for our contribution to a project. He may have even claimed credit for our work before his own superiors. In our minds, we now label the boss as untrustworthy and as an adversary.

When a partner in a romantic relationship decides they can't continue the affair, the other partner often feels abandoned, betrayed and utterly desolated. This trauma can lead to "total cascade failure" of a person with a poor self-image who is ruled principally by fear of loss. They might even murder their ex-lover, their kids and then perhaps themselves. Almost monthly such incidents appear in the newspaper and on the TV news.

Though for most people a romantic breakup or divorce doesn't lead to homicide, even so, the feeling of betrayal and abandonment may continue many years or even decades after the break up. It generalizes itself in the mind of the abandoned party to encompass their changed worldview of all men or women. They may feel that nobody can be trusted and that everybody is out for themselves. They try to insulate themselves from further pain by abandoning hope, feeling that anyone will betray anyone else if the price is right or the going gets too rough. The idea of love becomes a cruel joke to them. They may also come to feel that they are unworthy of anyone's romantic love.

These reactions to the boss and to the former lover do not serve us. Once again, that is the question to ask ourselves when emotion and/or fear of loss overcomes our rational mind.

Let's look at a more productive attitude towards betrayal and abandonment, because no matter what, so long as our hearts keep beating, we simply have to keep on *keeping on,* don't we?

Holding onto past injustices, transgressions and the spiritual toxin of hate

A survivor of a World War Two Japanese prisoner of war camp periodically visited the local veteran's hospital. He knew that his generation of World War Two survivors was passing into history. At the hospital, he came upon a veteran who had also been in a Japanese prisoner of war camp.

The conditions and treatment in the POW camp were, as you might expect, horrific. The Japanese code of bushido demanded that a soldier never surrender but fight to the death.

So the Japanese saw a prisoner as a dishonorable, sub-human coward. Torture and summary executions of prisoners by the Japanese was common in the work camps in Burma and elsewhere. Many prisoners died of disease, malnutrition and brutal forced labor.

The two POW camp survivors talked about the past and the Japanese POW camps. Before he left, the visiting veteran asked his new friend if he had forgiven the Japanese. The other veteran replied angrily that he would never forgive them.

His comrade said, "Then somehow they have still found a way to keep a part of you imprisoned in that camp." He was trying to show the other POW survivor that hatred did not serve him. He used his friend's hatred of the Japanese as a motivation to change his mindset to one that did serve him. He pointed out that as long as the man kept a burning hatred in his heart for the Japanese POW guards, they had still won over him even 55 years later!

The veteran also used all the fundamental principles of successful sales to help enlightenment of his newfound friend. The job of sales so often comes down to effective human communication and an understanding of the other's true problem.

Dealing rationally and productively with perceived betrayal or abuse in the office environment

Casting the boss in the role of an adversary does not serve one. It is difficult or impossible to be productive or to advance and be happy in your work if you feel this way about your superiors. After all, you must deal with them personally and perhaps daily. You would do better to express your feelings toward your boss and get it off your chest, and hopefully you can reach a better understanding of each other. Not to speak out is also showing a "bully boss" that you are a suitable victim that can be abused without redress.

Let's look at how this may be accomplished. The employee sets up a time to meet privately with the boss. At this meeting, the employee expresses an evaluation of what has occurred that they feel disturbed about.

Employee: "Mr. Johnston, we both worked on the Steiner analysis, didn't we?"

Boss: "Yes. You did a good job on that report."

Employee: "I am happy to hear you say that now, because that directly relates to what occurred at the corporate meeting. My contribution was not even mentioned, and that made me feel like you did not fully recognize my work. Since you did not mention my contribution at the meeting, the others certainly could not have recognized or appreciated it. I would feel much better if the next time we are in a presentation that you acknowledge my work on the presentation and analysis. I know that it is your position as executive director to present these reports. But I also feel that there is nothing incompatible with that responsibility of yours and what I am requesting."

Dealing with problem co-workers is still selling, and all the fundamental rules of sales apply.

The objective in talking to the boss was to sell the boss on the idea that it would be better for them if the boss acknowledged the employee's contribution. When the World War Two veteran told his new friend that he had allowed his hate to still "imprison" him, he was trying to sell the man on a healthier and more productive way of thinking about this terrible wartime experience and to let go of his hate. Both the employee and the war veteran were trying to sell something, and in both cases it was an idea and a new way of thinking.

What is the first objection to any sale that we must be prepared to deal with? The first objection is "no need." That is, I don't need your idea, service or solution, because I do not have the problem it is supposed to solve.

In the case of the employee versus the boss, this can be internalized in the boss's mind as, "This is not my problem, it is yours." Consequently, the boss may try to avoid meeting with the employee. He may expect the problem to go away, and he may try to ignore it. You must prepare for any sale, and so you need to anticipate the objections before you try to change anyone's mind about anything. Let's imagine the boss says, "I am very busy today. I'm sorry but this will just have to wait."

You will recognize this objection as the "no need" objection. It sounds like the "no hurry" objection, and to an extent it is, but its real basis is that the boss does not see that *he* has a problem. The boss feels that there is no real need to meet with you.

Show him that there is a problem, that it is a problem involving him, and that there is a need for him to solve it by meeting with you. So just say: "I know you are very busy, Mr. Smith. That goes with your job and I respect that, but we have a problem here and we need to solve it. To do that we need to meet in private and very soon. Can we agree to meet at 5:00 p.m. today in your office?"

Do you see that as simple as this statement is, it covers many bases? But, also realize that if you had not thought out what you were going to say beforehand and had not anticipated the boss's objection to meeting with you, then you might have been caught "flat footed" and choked and said nothing. But by pre-defining your goals, your choices will become much easier and the proper tactics more apparent.

First, you have given the boss his "props." "I know you are busy. That goes with your job, and I respect that."

Second, you stated that there was a problem and that it was his problem as well as yours. "We have a problem here, and we need to solve it."

Third, you made a specific proposal and asked for his agreement to that proposal, and thus you forced a decision from him. This was a decision he thought he could postpone or dismiss when he said, "I am very busy today. I'm sorry but this will have to wait."

In doing this, you did not allow the negotiations to begin with you in a clearly subordinate position. At the same time you were not insubordinate either. You gave the boss his "props."

For a person with a positive self-image and experience in negotiating, most of the elements of sales start to come naturally and freely. Conversely, a person with an uncertain self-image or who is given to constant self-criticism and irrational fears will have a difficult time in persuading anyone to their point of view. They often fall back on emotional arguments, which amplify their insecurity and are non-productive, because emotional responses do not define their goal in the negotiation.

The futility and counter-productive nature of personal emotional "arguments" in office negotiations

For example, the employee might come to the boss in anger, perhaps even showing pain (imagine if they were actually sobbing!) and say, "Mr. Smith, I am shocked and hurt at how you ignored my contribution to the report in the meeting! How could you do such a thing?"

Emotional venting would damage the employee's credibility with the boss. And for some bosses, it would identify the employee as someone they could emotionally manipulate for their own ends.

The emotional outburst challenges the boss' authority and perhaps even his competence. It denies him his props and might make him aggressively defensive. The emotional approach also does not project the problem as one shared by the boss either. It identifies the problem as the employee being "very hurt."

Finally, this emotional approach makes no proposal that demands a decision or an agreement with the boss. In effect, it is more of a personal attack: "How could you do such a thing?"

We will not fall into these counter-productive, reactive mind, non-communication traps if we think ahead and plan our communication strategies. Planning includes the following:

1) Clearly define your goal beforehand. What do you want at this stage of the negotiation, and how will you know when it has been conceded to you?

2) Define a secondary goal if the first is unattainable at the time of the negotiation. For example, if the boss responds that he cannot meet with you at 5:00 p.m., ask him when he can meet. If he says he will get back to you, suggest a time and ask for his agreement.

3) Anticipate which of the three types of objections to the sale (no need, no help, or no hurry) will likely be the central objection. In your own mind, play the part of the other party and articulate those objections. Rehearse a plan and the verbiage to defuse those objections or to dissolve them or to blend with them so that you can redirect them.

4) Prepare a proposal that demands a decision and solicits an agreement from the other party and which brings you a step closer to your ultimate goal in the negotiation.

The essential value and the necessity of forgiveness

Forgiveness does not mean that you accept the harmful act—real or perceived—of another. Indeed, forgiveness is not even an unselfish act in itself, because it is not exclusively for the offending party. It is for YOU.

Forgiveness is a sharp tool that we should polish to a fine edge. Forgiveness severs the burdens that we might otherwise carry from the transgressions of others. Forgiveness is the transformation of your own heart so that you release the pain and resentment over the wrongs that someone has done to you. It can also be self-forgiveness over an act you have done that abused or diminished another or yourself. In fact, you cannot abuse another's spirit without degrading your own as well.

The objective of true forgiveness is to purify yourself from the negative emotional baggage that you might otherwise carry with you for years. But you cannot genuinely forgive yourself for your own acts until you accept and acknowledge your responsibility for them and then try to redress them as far as possible.

Consider the World War Two veteran who could never forgive the Japanese. Was the other veteran trying to show him that he should do so for the sake of the Japanese? No. Was he condoning what the Japanese did in the POW camp? Most certainly not!

He was trying to show his comrade that he was punishing *himself* with his hatred of the Japanese and that he had been doing so for 55 years. He was trying to show the man that he needed to let go of his hatred *for his own sake*—not for the sake of the Japanese.

We must let go of hatreds, resentments, or jealousies. They are emotional baggage that burden us. Forgiveness is one of the most powerful tools we have in our arsenal to change our worldview and enhance our self-image, and we must us it. Indeed, try to practice the art of forgiveness daily.

I try to do this, for example, when a driver pulls out in front of me and forces me to slow down abruptly to avoid rear-ending him. However, sometimes the best I can do is the following self-dialogue: "You stupid son of a bitch! Well, I am not going to let your stupidity change my mood. I am going to just relax, breath deeply and let go of this negative feeling right now and remain happy; God bless me."

My hope, through effort, is that I will do better than this in the future. Even so, the essential idea of forgiveness—not internalizing the negative experience and carrying it with you inside like a poison—is still there even in my semi-maniacal self-dialogue above.

Anger comes from fear or pain.

If we increase our mental awareness, we can see the very things that make us angry *before* they have the full "anger" effect on us.

Anger arises from either fear or from a sense that another is hurting us. Fear and hurt can co-mingle and are sometimes even difficult to differentiate from one another.

Think about an event that made you angry. Didn't the feeling of hurt or fear precede the anger? Irrational anger is a voice inside that tells us where and how and when we have been trapped into a totally reactive mind-set. It shows us how and where the world has hijacked control of our consciousness and perhaps even our rationality.

The role of anger in physical self-defense

There are times when anger is the emotion that serves us best, though. For example, when one is forced to fight physically to defend themselves, then anger is the best most people can ever do to actualize their survival instincts and energize their defense.

But, from deeper experience in dealing with physical violence, I can say that there is an even more effective mechanism than anger. I have difficulty describing this mental state in words other than "a relaxed but focused and resolute intent in mind and body."

Anger in a physical fight is like a fierce fire. It burns itself out quickly. Anger is also somewhat blind. This itself is OK, however, as a real physical fight does not last long as a rule. The outcome of most hand-to-hand fights is decided in the first seconds of the engagement. Therefore, anger is a functional response to direct physical aggression and can assist greatly in one's efforts at self-defense.

Please stay with me on this extended metaphor, as what I am talking about here does not apply only to physical battle. It is just that I have some experience in physical combat.

The value of meeting aggression without irrational fear

As I have said, in my bar work I learned that I could—and that I must—remain relaxed even as people threw punches at me or tried to hit me with beer bottles. Experience in that environment made it clear to me that *if* I could relax but also maintain a very fluid and yet very focused mind and intent towards my assailant, then I could sometimes defeat large and aggressive attackers. The assailants were totally consumed with hatred and anger. Indeed, I used their anger and hatred to work against them, which allowed me to "enter" upon them. To accomplish this demanded that I let go of my irrational fears and engage a non-reactive mind-set.

Putting this same idea another way, I learned that the more fear I allowed to reside within me before or during the battle, the more likely I was to get hurt. In addition, having a relaxed, focused mind and displaying an absence of fear was sometimes "read" by the potential assailant. This was often enough to discourage him from trying his luck at assaulting me as a bouncer.

Fear would have slowed my body by tensing my muscles. I would have had to overcome that tension before I could move those muscles and limbs to strike or slip a blow. Fear can also slow or stop our minds from engaging in rational thought as well. Remember, I am talking exclusively about irrational fear, not the survival instinct generated by gut feelings that we are in physical danger. To feel fear in the face of a potential physical attack is normal and functional. That is rational fear. I just had a special opportunity as a bouncer to get somewhat past that response.

Consequently, if you happen to be a martial artist or want to acquire superior self-defense ability, please let me add this caution. I was able to get to the point where I could let go of fear and move fast and fluidly only because I was forced to get used to being attacked for real. I got past being overcome by the adrenal rush and began to manage and to use it productively.

It is not likely that this state of mind can be achieved by any traditional martial arts training methods that I am aware of, though. That is why, building on the work of others, I began to develop the RMCAT self-defense adrenal stress conditioning training technology.

So do not misunderstand me here. For most all of us, martial artist or not, anger and a 110% commitment to a ruthless defense is going to be our best and most available strategy in a real attack. But a physical attack, though we should prepare for it, is not what most of us will have to deal with. Yet the same principle of the value of a non-reactive mind still holds true in any stressful situation. If we can relax when a boss or other person is berating us, challenging our competence, or even threatening us, then we often take the wind out of the attacker's sails.

Further, being relaxed and in "non-reactive mind" and yet focused, we are far less likely to internalize into our own self-dialogues and self-images the discord being projected our way. The non-reactive mind-set response often discourages the person from trying to "rattle" you further, as they have experienced the frustration of having their strategy fail. They won't often try to get your goat again unless they think up a new way to break through your calm rationality.

For someone to be able to push, there must be something to push against.

CHAPTER REVIEW

1) Our minds have a significant effect over our bodies and our health. A Russian proverb sums up this idea: "The brain can have a conversation with the body that ends in death." Constant stress puts significant strain on our hearts. This can lead to a heart attack or stroke. Depression lowers the strength of our immune system. This can lead to periodic colds or other pathologies that we might otherwise have resisted had we not impaired our immunity through negative self-dialogue and depression.

2) We do not always recognize the level of chronic stress we are under. This is because in severely stressful situations, we direct our minds to sublimate the stress so that we can function in that environment. But like a soldier who has spent months on a battlefield, a point can come where the energy needed to maintain this sublimation fails. Then the soldier can have a catastrophic mental failure. For the soldier this might express itself as a fully catatonic state. This failure may motivate the frustrated postal worker or other office or warehouse worker to get a gun and demonstrate that he is not powerless and that he will have retribution against his "transgressors" by committing multiple homicides. While these are the extreme cases, failure to manage stress properly is still always destructive to out mental and physical health.

3) Often, it is only when we are removed from a high stress situation that we can gauge the true intensity of the destructive effect stress has had on our mind and body.

4) Stress affects our heart and blood pressure. Have your blood pressure measured by a physician and then by the wrist devices available today. High blood pressure can usually be controlled with appropriate drugs, but not if the condition goes undetected too long. High blood pressure can be a result of high stress, and if left untreated it can kill.

5) Some persons are hyper responders to adrenal events. It appears that hyper response can be missed in standard blood pressure and heart exams since there is too little stress in the doctor's office to elicit the hyper response. If you are a hyper responder, you may be at cardiovascular risk, and you need to discover if this is the case. A cardiac physician can perform a stress analysis test of your heart function.

6) Behaviors found in hyper responders, and to a lesser extent with normal adrenal responders too, include (a) Road rage (b) Impatience and difficulty standing in lines (c) A strong aversion to being in large crowds. In general, impatience with others that frequently leads to anger (particularly in stressful situations) is a common behavioral trait with hyper responders. In contrast, some hyper responders will freeze up under even mild adrenal stress.

7) Our emotions are not automatic; they are not simply the fixed result of a given event. Our emotions are in great part determined by how we interpret that event. If we can change our interpretation of the event, we can reduce the stress we experience as a result of that event. For example, through rational self-dialogue, we can tell ourselves that the people wasting our time in the fast food line are simply oblivious and that they do not intend to anger or disrespect or control us. When someone says something that angers or saddens us or hurts us or seems to be an indictment of our abilities, we need to pause and examine what they really said. We need to think about how our previous conditioning and the emotional "baggage" we are carrying colors our initial, gut level feeling about what they said. We can easily misunderstand what a person says if we are "primed" to hear an indictment of our abilities or self-worth. Next, we need to consider how much that person's opinion means to us anyway, and why. The person who habitually tries to cast us into a lesser role of competence than themselves often does so because of their own feelings of inadequacy. Associating with such people does not serve us, and we should consider removing their negative influence from our lives.

8) We need to realize that we see every event and action through the "glass darkly" of our own personal worldview. This basic worldview is first developed in us as children. It is given to us by our parents or other guardians as well as other childhood and adolescent experiences. But one's worldview is not fixed and immutable; you can change it to a more functional one that serves you better. However, to begin to do so we must first define the key attitudes that constitute our existing worldview. Where did they come from? How functional or realistic are they? How do they serve us? When do they fail us and complicate our lives? Non-functional worldviews can lead to fixed ideas about how people and the world should or MUST be. This is self-defeating. Everyone will simply not fit into your worldview.

9) We need to understand cognitive dissonance and reaction formation to restructure our worldviews. Cognitive dissonance is the stress and conflict we experience when we hold two directly opposing concepts of the world. The worldview that "Everybody will be nice to you if you're nice to them" is a non-functional worldview. That worldview will cause mental conflict that is exaggerated beyond what it has to be. This is inevitable since we certainly will encounter people who are "not nice." We can begin to modify this worldview to a more functional, less stress-inducing one, by changing our self-dialogue. For example, we might say to ourselves, "Many people are basically nice. But not everyone is, and it would be unrealistic of me to expect everyone to be nice, or for all people to behave as I would want. I will not allow the mean people to bring down my own self-confidence or self-image. People who are destructive and abusive of others are always suffering from a damaged and unsure self-image. I should not let that affect my feelings about the world or myself."

Reaction formation occurs when we generalize, going from the specific to the universal. For example, one person betrays us in a romantic love affair. We might then fall into the reaction formation and defensive thinking such as "All men are really pigs" or "All women are deceitful and will betray any man if they think the circumstances are right for them." This is an attempt to create a defensive insulation from the pain of the failed affair. After all, if we convince ourselves that no woman or man can really be trusted in romance, then there is no use worrying about it or expecting fidelity. Indeed, reaction formation can drive other romantic partners into the same betrayal or abandonment. Reaction formation is not often done consciously, though. Ironically, reaction formation is done partly to escape the cognitive dissonance of someone who does not seem to fit an "all men/women are swine" worldview.

10) Venting emotionally over a perceived transgression from an office co-worker, a boss or even a marital partner is not effective communication. But sometimes we may actually need to vent our anger and disappointment by giving it voice and strong articulation. Yet, in an office situation the ineffectiveness of emotional venting is quite clear. For example, a boss fails to give credit to an employee or takes credit for the employee's work, and the employee comes to the boss shouting, "Damn it Mr. Jones, what you did was absolutely unforgivable and I am deeply offended!" This is self-defeating for that employee. The employee has taken ownership of the problem. That is, the employee has expressed the problem as "I am hurt." Thus, the boss can dismiss the emotional outburst as a "non-problem" for him or her. It is the employee's emotional problem and not the boss'. It is far more effective not to engage in emotional display in the office. We should wait until we are composed and then plan our communication strategy, which should include the following:

a) A clearly defined goal.

b) A secondary goal if the first is not attainable at the time of the communication.

c) Anticipation of likely objections to obtaining that goal and a logical plan to overcome those objections.

d) In any negotiation, we should have a specific proposal that demands a decision from the other party and solicits an agreement.

11) We must recognize the tremendous value of forgiveness. The act of forgiveness is the personal resolution that we will not carry the poison within us from the hurtful actions of another. It does not mean we condone the act of injury or cruelty. Forgiveness means that we have resolved to let go of the dark toxicity of the event for our own happiness and that we will waste none of our precious life's energy on hate or pointless vengeance or chronic melancholy over the past. The past is just that, and it is unchangeable. But your future can be what you determine to make it.

12) If we can develop the ability to meet aggression without displaying fear—be it the threat of physical aggression, the simple pushiness or rudeness of an office worker, or casual street or supermarket line conflict—then we have put ourselves into a mental position that is tactically superior to that of our opposition. In some cases the opposition will perceive our self-confidence and our mental calmness. This may discourage them from continuing. If it is a physical fight, this is the best mental state, because it allows us to see everything that is about to occur and to move instantly and fluidly as demanded.

Drug, Alcohol and Tobacco Addiction

Drug and alcohol abuse including cocaine, heroin and pre-scription drug addiction are almost rampant in our stress-laden society. The medical community often refers to such addicted persons as being "self medicating."

Depression—a feeling of worthlessness or that life itself is pointless—is sometimes the central factor that drives persons to try to escape through substance abuse. Hence, we can see how the inverse of these same factors—a strong personal self-image and a realistic but optimistic worldview—are very important elements in resisting or escaping from substance abuse.

On the most basic level, people abuse prescription drugs, al-cohol, or use illegal drugs like cocaine or heroin to feel good without having to do anything. This is a simple explanation, but if you ponder it a bit, you might also see how true it is.

What is it that usually makes us feel good about our lives and ourselves? In general it is personal accomplishment: solv-ing a problem, building an addition to your home, advancing in your career, finding love, or raising a child. All of these make us feel good about ourselves, because they reaffirm and strengthen our positive and competent self-image.

Yet none of these accomplishments are possible without *ef-fort and risk,* are they? Finding love, for example, is certainly not without great emotional exposure and risk. Genuine posi-tive feelings such as these are not achieved without effort. You have to *do something* and often risk something. This is the se-duction of substance abuse: You just take the "happiness pill" to feel "good" and to escape feeling bad. But substance abuse is a lie. It is self-destructive.

This is not just anecdotal information for me, either. In in-vestigating the modus operandi of criminals, I have dealt with a number of persons addicted to heroin and other substances or who were formerly addicted. Some of them I got to know well.

It is not the drug alone that causes the disintegration of a person's life.

Now let's look at something a bit more complex regarding opiate and opiate-like drug addictions. Some physicians, though only a small minority, are addicted to morphine or other prescription drugs. Yet these doctors can be very functional. They maintain a proper diet, and they do not have a totally failed self-image either. In fact, they often have a very high opinion of themselves.

They also use pure pharmaceutical-grade drugs, so they do not damage their health with the adulterants found in illegal street drugs. They always use fresh, sterile needles too (if they inject their drug of choice, but few do inject their drugs). They may eventually be discovered, but they perform reasonably well as physicians even for long periods while also being addicted to morphine or other substances. Physician addiction is certainly not limited to morphine, either.

The point here is that once again we can see how important our personal self-image is to our health and well-being both physically and emotionally. Physicians in general have a very strong sense of accomplishment and in some cases even a subdued feeling of superiority over others. Because of this, they respect themselves and are more likely to take decent care of themselves physically.

Hence, with the strong and positive self-image factor going for them, they remain functional and productive for some time even after becoming morphine addicts.

In contrast to the street addict, you are not going to find the physician robbing liquor stores to support his habit. You will not find him looking like the hollowed-out shell of a malnourished heroin addict street person either. You will find him in a fine restaurant with his lovely wife and morphine coursing through his veins at just the appropriate level. So it is not the drug alone that causes the total cascade failure of a morphine or heroin addict.

It is the total collapse and the abandonment of a person's own sense of personal self-worth that ultimately destroys the addict, and not the drug alone. The drug abuse is to some extent a symptom of their lack of self value. Addiction to the drug greatly exacerbates that problem too.

Functional alcoholics

There is a continuum of addiction to substance abuse. There are many functional alcoholics in our society, and some of them are very successful CEOs of major corporations too. Alcoholism is fairly widespread and is not limited to the stereotypic image of the "wino" drinking from the paper bag on the street.

A good number of alcoholics have no idea that they are alcoholics. Also, two people might drink the same amount of alcohol, but one may be addicted while the other is not.

Alcoholism damages the heart muscles, and with chronic, long-term use, it will damage the liver and kidneys. Cirrhosis of the liver is a common cause of death from chronic alcoholism. But of course, marriages, careers, and health can fall along the wayside first.

As in the example of the addicted physician, the addict's personal sense of self-worth and achievement, if it is held intact, can sometimes even alter (or postpone) the truly abysmal fate of drug addicts. It should also be obvious that a person who respects himself and carries a strong internal personal self-image is less likely to succumb to drug addiction. But we need to realize that such a person is certainly not immune to such addiction, either. None of us is a perfect human being, and even if we were, then we would never fit in *anywhere* in our imperfect social order, would we?

How addicts have successfully freed themselves from addictions

The major change in the reformed addicts I have dealt with has always been some factor that enhanced or otherwise provided them with a renewed sense of personal self-worth. Sometimes religion did this. Sometimes Narcotics Anonymous or Alcoholics Anonymous groups gave them the cognitive tools and the group support to escape their addictive lifestyles. But the common element in every successful recovery from drug addiction that I have ever seen has been an elevated and renewed sense of personal self-worth.

With this elevated sense of self-worth comes the thought, the belief and the hope in the addict that they can change. The idea that change is possible enters the mind. I have actually seen that moment, that illumination of spirit and liberation of mind. One addict said to me, "It was like a light bulb went on in my head. I don't have to go to prison anymore, I can raise my children, and I don't have to take heroin just to feel normal."

I have discussed drug and alcohol addiction here not only because it is dangerous and destructive. I use it to illustrate the great power of how we organize our minds. How we organize our thinking and our worldview and our view of ourselves can bring a great and positive change in our lives.

Think about it: If a heroin addict or a hard-core alcoholic can escape their terrible and powerfully destructive drug addiction by reorganizing their self-view and worldview, imagine what you might accomplish by doing the same!

Our personality and genetic make-up interact in complex ways.

Recall the two soldiers who received nearly identical superficial wounds. One died from his wound, and the other just kept on moving and lived.

Consider two war veterans who experienced basically the same horrors of combat. One veteran returned with a severe and disabling case of Post Traumatic Stress Syndrome while the other went through a period of readjustment and then lived a normal and productive life.

Some of the differences in these cases have to do with the way these individuals were raised. That affected the formation of their initial worldviews and their personal self-esteem and self-image. However, there are other factors at work here. One of the determinants in how we might behave in a given circumstance is locked into our individual genetic code. The interaction between our fixed genetic structures and our personal psychology (which includes our mutable worldview and personal self-image and sense of self-worth) is very complex and not well understood.

The role of genetics versus the way one is raised is sometimes referred to as the classic "nature versus nurture" debate. A child raised in a multilingual home, for example, will usually learn both languages easily and naturally. As adults they become fluent native speakers of both languages. If that same individual were raised in a single-language environment, it would be far, far more difficult for them to learn a second language as an adult.

This is because the brain wiring that accepts language acquisition is very mutable as a child. Once a language is acquired as a child, it seems to pre-empt the natural neural pathways for additional language acquisition because of the installation of that first language.

The point is that whatever the biochemical and neurological mechanisms are at work here, it is apparent that some of the neural centers of our brains are dedicated or at least pre-disposed for storing specific control logic for certain motor functions or cognitive skills. And yet there are some people who can pick up a number of additional languages easily as adults. I know such a person: Dr. Alan R. Micholson, whom I worked with in undergraduate school. He travels extensively around the world now, and he picks up a new language in just three or four weeks.

Hence, nature (or personal genetics) and nurture (our personal experiences and childhood upbringing) interact together in a myriad of mysterious ways. Yet even our physical brain wiring does not seem to be immutable. A person who suffers an accident or stroke that damages some neurological motor control system can sometimes, through arduous physical therapy, regain some measure of control by learning to use other neural pathways.

This effort does not occur at a fully self-aware level, of course. It is the "body" that learns to move the limb or the speech apparatus through the alternative pathways. Though this is extreme, here we have yet another example of how an individual can change his or her own brain wiring.

We cannot change the genetics we were born with, but we can make significant change in our modalities of thinking and thus the way we respond to life's trials and disappointments. We might be genetically predisposed to alcoholism, for example. There exists a very clear and statistically significant research to suggest that there is a genetic link involved in alcoholism. Yet, we can make the personal decision to abstain from alcohol, and if so, then we will never become alcoholics, will we? In that case, our genetic predisposition becomes almost irrelevant. In fact, I believe that a person with a genetic predisposition to alcoholism might, in some cases, have a drink and still avoid becoming an alcoholic.

On the other hand, some people must not have that drink. Total abstinence from any alcohol is their only path to escape from alcohol addiction. This is the position of AAA (Alcoholics Anonymous Association). The AAA is without doubt the most effective organization I know of in helping people liberate themselves from alcohol addiction.

It is true that a great deal of our personality, our image of ourselves, and our worldview is formed during our early childhood. But while we can't change our childhood, we can still modify and change our worldview and our personal self-image. A parent that tells a child "You ain't worth a damn" will have an effect on the kid. But the parent telling the kid that he is "not worth a damn" *does not make it so, does it?* That child or later that adult can change their self-perception and in doing so change their lives so very much for the better.

We cannot leave this subject of brain biochemistry and the use of drugs without addressing what appears to be an advance in the treatment of chronic depression and such things as obsessive/compulsive disorder. I refer to the SSRI family of drugs (selective serotonin reuptake inhibitors). These drugs are somewhat controversial, especially Prozac.

How SSRI drugs came into being

Starting around the 1970s, anti-depressant drugs were designed based on our knowledge (which is still in its adolescence) of human brain chemistry. Before that, the discovery of anti-depressant drugs was often the result of the chance observation of patients who were being treated for pathologies other than depression.

Iproniazid is a drug used to treat tuberculosis. When it was observed that TB patients taking the drug experienced an anti-depressant effect, the chemistry of Iproniazid was studied further, and it eventually became a tool for the treatment of depression.

Serotonin is one of several chemicals that serve as "chemical messengers" between one brain cell and another. There are at least fifty known neurotransmitter chemicals that serve as these "messengers" in our brains. Brain chemistry is extraordinarily complex since these agents seem to work in concert. It is believed that when one drug is used to treat one neurotransmitter, it must have some effect on all the others.

Even so, serotonin levels in the brain seem to be of particular significance in persons with depression, anxiety disorders, obsessive/compulsive disorders, sleep problems and other behavioral problems.

Depression is a fairly serious clinical pathology that affects the lives of a great many people in our society. It is quite apparent that clinical depression is not "all in one's head" either, yet our self-attitudes and worldview can affect the severity of depression and how we handle it. But clinical depression also seems to be a matter of brain chemistry imbalance.

Do we really understand how SSRI's work?

Many of us would like to believe that doctors have well-established and proven reasons for selecting the drugs they prescribe and that they understand exactly how and why the drugs work. But this is not the case. The neurochemistry of the way Selective Serotonin Re-Uptake Inhibitors (SSRI's) work is not fully understood. Since I am not even a physician, I will limit my discussion of these drugs to what is generally accepted and also to my personal experience in taking them myself.

The basic concept in SSRI's is to reduce the amount of re-absorption of serotonin that is issued by neurotransmitter cells. To simplify it, the idea is to get the "message" through. This is why this class of drugs is called Selective Serotonin Re-Uptake Inhibitors. A key word here is "selective." SSRI's do not work for everyone, nor does the same SSRI work for everyone in the same manner.

One SSRI like Zoloft may have the desired effect on one person and not on another. However, switching to another drug, like Paxil or some other SSRI, may achieve that desired beneficial effect for that individual.

For example, the SSRI Celexa caused me to feel even greater anxiety, but Paxil evened out my moods and elevated me from periods of depression. These are not miracle drugs, but I do feel they are useful for *some* persons suffering from depression and to a lesser extend other behavioral disorders.

All SSRI's will take a minimum of about five days to as much as a month or more to begin to have their full effect. The main SSRI brand names in the US are Prozac, Paxil, Zoloft, Luvox and Celexa.

My personal experience with Paxil

Once again we must keep in mind that a particular SSRI that is effective for one person may not have that same or even similar effect on another person. Our individual brain chemistries are simply that—our own *individual* brain chemistries. But I will relate how I found Paxil to be beneficial.

First, I feel I should explain why I felt the need to take an SSRI in the first place. It was because I came to realize that I was experiencing periodic intervals of true depression for which I had no explanation.

My business was going very well. I had achieved many of my personal career goals. My work was having a major and positive impact on the martial arts world and the entire self-defense training industry, and not only in the United States, but in Europe and elsewhere. After a long struggle, my concepts in this field regarding the effects of adrenal stress training had ultimately demonstrated themselves to be useful and they were now being recognized and employed by some of the highest-placed professionals in this small and special industry.

In addition, my financial status was very good at that point in time (much better than it is now actually), and not just from my self-defense instructional programs either. The stock market was doing very well for me during that period, and my personal portfolio was doing extremely well.

My marriage is quite important to me, and my wife and I were getting along fine just as we had for many years. Even so, I was aware of my wife's tension over my unexpected and unexplainable depressive behaviors. Even though I seemed to have lot going for me, I nonetheless had periods of real depression that would last for months. I could not find the source or reason for this depression. I knew I felt it, but it did not seem logical to me. I felt that the way things were going, I should be as happy as the proverbial clam, but I was not.

I began to drink more alcohol too. I lost interest in some of the things that had given me satisfaction and recreation. I knew that all of these were the classical signs of clinical depression. Consequently, I consulted a physician to determine if I had some definitive, organic malady that could explain this depression. My doctor confirmed that I was experiencing the textbook signs of depression. He informed me that a large percentage of adults, perhaps as many as 40%, experienced unexplainable periods of depression such as mine at some point in their lives.

Ultimately his argument for my taking an SSRI came down to this: "What you are doing now isn't working for you, is it?"

He was correct. I needed to try something else in addition to my own self-cognitive and somewhat "self-medicating" approach. Yet I was reluctant to take drugs that would directly affect my brain and thinking. I was even a bit concerned over news stories about people going homicidally berserk on SSRI's like Prozac.

Further, I cannot deny than mine has not been the "ordinary" life in that I have been conditioned to a much higher level of physical violence than most people. Because of this, these media stories of Prozac patients going "bonkers" concerned me even more.

Yet I realized that I was already given to occasional bursts of violence, not directed against people but against objects, like throwing a champagne glass through a window in a momentary fit of anger. This was not normal or acceptable behavior for me. This behavior did not serve me, and I wanted to eliminate it or at least better control it somehow.

As I studied the documented episodes of persons losing control on SSRI's and getting violent or suicidal on Prozac, I saw that most of them were male teenagers. Further, almost all of them went "berserk" only after they had discontinued the drug without their physician's knowledge. It appeared that there was risk of Prozac withdrawal for some people.

The subject cases that had violence problems with the SSRI's were young males, and I also knew that the high levels of the hormone testosterone could be like a temporary "madness" in and of itself for a teenage boy. I recall one of my professors joking to me many years ago, "What's the difference between a teenaged boy and a sociopath?" His answer was, "About 8 to 10 years."

At age 54, I felt that I was safer from the potential side effects of violent behavior than those few teenage male subjects I had read about. But this was just a feeling that was not backed up by any controlled, scientific research as far as I knew.

My doctor prescribed Paxil, a newer drug than Prozac. After about three or four weeks of taking Paxil, my wife informed me that I was much more upbeat and positive. My outbursts of violence like throwing the champagne glass ended as well. I had greater patience with people. I no longer felt the chronic depression.

Please understand that the drug was not a "happiness pill" for me at all. It simply seemed to correct my brain chemistry and to make me more myself. There is no high or euphoria associated with taking SSRI's, at least as far as I have experienced.

Because I had a better and more positive attitude, I also became more productive in my work, so I became more satisfied with myself. I felt my actions and behaviors were now more congruent with what I like to perceive as my own, positive self-image. I was just more "me" again.

Negative side effects of SSRI's

First, let's keep in mind that the new SSRI's are not cure-alls for *anything*. In fact, in a large Danish medical study it was shown that SSRI's were less effective than the older tricyclic (Clomipramine) in patients with very severe depression. The Danish tricyclic patients were hospitalized though, while most SSRI patients are treated on an outpatient basis here in the United States. I feel that this fact *may* have had some impact on the study's findings, too. Perhaps the severity of the Danish in-patients' depression was too great for the SSRI's to help. It is also possible that the SSRI outpatients in the US may have unknowingly skewed some of the outpatient data, since that data came chiefly from the SSRI patients themselves.

I can confidently say that Paxil has been beneficial for me, though. However, these drugs do have side effects that are experienced to various degrees. Some people experience dry mouth, gastric disturbances (stomach pains), sleepiness, and greater passivity. Sexual side effects may include loss or reduced interest in sex or difficulty in achieving an orgasm. Some newer SSRI's are reported to reduce or eliminate these negative sexual side effects. Wellbutrin is such a drug that seems to have no negative sexual side effects, but it has had the problem in its first trials of causing seizures in a small minority of patients.

Even so, Wellbutrin is again making progress in the marketplace now. I feel that this is because of its reported absence of sexual side effects. Wellbutrin sometimes causes anxiety and insomnia in some people. But then this is true for some individuals with any particular SSRI. Consider my own higher anxiety reaction to the SSRI Celexa.

The only way you will know which if any of these new drugs will help you is to consult a physician who has experience prescribing them. You should be prepared for some experimentation, some trial and error, before the physician prescribes the particular SSRI that is most beneficial for you.

The Hawthorne Effect: the importance of attitude in productivity

People, as a rule, want to feel better. They also want and need to feel special. That is why placebos (sugar pills or other fake "drugs") can actually have a positive effect.

There is a famous study that was done many decades ago that resulted in the term "Hawthorne Effect." This term is used to describe the positive result of people being made more productive only because they thought they were in a special test group. The special test group differed from the control group by the employment of some device—drug or other technology—not used in the control group.

In the Hawthorne study, workers were told that a new type of light was going to be installed in their factory assembly area. They were told that these new lights would reduce their eyestrain and mental fatigue and thus allow them to work more efficiently and to be more productive.

They were told that the other assembly building next to their own (the control group) would not receive the new lighting in order to serve as a baseline of comparison to their own special, new experimental lighting group. Other than that, the control group was identical.

In fact, *the productivity of the test group did improve* over that of the control group. It can be assumed that the special test group really did feel special too. After all, *they* were chosen to receive the new improved lighting over the control group. But in reality, there was no difference at all between the special group's "new lights" and the control group's old lights. The increased productivity of the special test group must have been the result of their feeling part of a special group.

But is this really any different than saying that their increased productivity was due to their enhanced self-images and sense of self-worth? I do not think so.

How we feel about ourselves simply affects everything we do in every arena of our life. We habitually must use our mental tools and awareness skills to develop a positive, optimistic, and yet realistic personal self-image and worldview.

We must come to believe and understand that we can do more than we at first think we might be capable of doing. Then we should act on those feelings. We must be guided more by hope than by fear. At the same time we must accept and be at peace with our limitations. But we must always be vigilant that we are not the architects of only perceived limitations either.

When we feel good about ourselves, others are much more likely to feel good about us too. Unfortunately, the converse is also true. Though I realize that this can easily be misinterpreted, I will go so far as to say that if we do not truly love and accept ourselves, then we will have great difficulty loving and accepting others. To love and accept ourselves, we need to peel away each defensive and self-deceptive layer of ourselves like we might peel away the layers of an onion.

We have to look inside and see what mechanisms we are maintaining to deceive ourselves from seeing what we would rather not admit about ourselves. We must identify a target before we can remove it. We can make no real progress on our journey of self-improvement if we lie to ourselves about who we are inside. No matter what it is we fear, we must see and accept that we are afraid *before* we can overcome that fear.

CHAPTER REVIEW

1) It is not dependence on the drug *alone* that destroys a drug addict. Even the strong physical addiction to heroin can usually be overcome in a week to ten days of painful withdrawal. But the psychological addiction will most often still remain very strong at the end of those several days of painful physical withdrawal. The addiction is a reflection of the addict's feelings of a failed and uncontrollable life for which escape is demanded. This can lead to the total cascade failure of

the addict's spirit and psyche. However, it is evident that the drug alone, in and of itself, does not solely create this situation. If that were the case, there would be no functional addicts of morphine, alcohol or other substances. It is apparent that to a degree, some addicts can function. The factor functional addicts seem to have in common is a positive self-image and sense of personal, professional accomplishment.

Nonetheless, a person with a strong personal self-image acts in a way that reflects genuine self-esteem. Hence, the development and maintenance of a positive self-image discourages drug abuse. Successful drug and alcohol rehabilitation programs employ this very principle— enhancing a person's sense of self-worth—to break their addiction. Such programs also give the recovering addict inclusion into a special and supportive peer group.

It has been shown that people who feel part of a special group outperform a control group, even though there is no real difference between the special group and the control group. This has been called the Hawthorne Effect after a classical industrial experiment. This psychological concept has long been used by the military in "special" units and special personnel nomenclature (i.e. lance corporal, specialist, etc.). The way a group thinks about itself is of key importance to their performance. This, of course, holds true on the individual level as well.

Our personalities, our behavior patterns, and our own genetic make-up are intertwined in a complex way. We cannot change our genetics, but we can change and augment our personal self-image and our worldviews. In this book we have presented some tools to do that, such as rationale self-talks and the positive identification of our self-defeating patterns of thought so that we can begin to let them go. Much of our fundamental worldview and self-image are formed in early childhood. But this does not pre-empt us from modifying these key personality elements. Indeed, understanding and accepting what our current worldview is based on and how these initial attitudes were first developed is a tool in achieving this positive change.

Depression is widespread in our stress-filled society. It is so prevalent that new drugs are being developed specifically for this pathology. Since about the 1970s a new class of drugs, Selective Serotonin Re-uptake Inhibitors (SSRI's) have been shown to be of value in the treatment of depression in some persons, and to a lesser extent, in helping people with obsessive/compulsive disorders. Finding the specific SSRI that might help you is somewhat a trial and error process. SSRI's effect different people in different ways. SSRI's do have negative sexual side effects. Newer SSRI's may succeed in avoiding these side effects.

If we can bring ourselves to a place where we are happy and accepting of ourselves, where we are directed more by hope than by fear, then we make it easier for others to be happy with us too. But, this feeling of self-worth must be genuine, and it must be predicated on reality. Our behaviors must be congruent with our positive self-image, or we are simply fooling ourselves.

It is best to cultivate a genuine, reasonably healthy (but not narcissistic) spiritual love and acceptance of ourselves in order to find and enjoy the rewards of the love of another. This demands that we first come to honestly know ourselves and see ourselves as we truly are. Then we must shed the excess baggage that does not serve, just as a snake might shed its old skin.

"A young man who does not fight and conquer has missed the best part of his youth, and an old man who does not know how to listen to the secrets of the brooks as they tumble down from the peaks to the valleys makes no sense. He is a spiritual mummy who is nothing but a rigid relic of the past." —Carl G. Jung

A night I will always remember

A few years ago I was strapped into a helicopter that had landed on my property in Colorado. I had suffered a heart attack in my sleep. The night was moonless and starless and as black as it could possibly be.

I could hear everything happening around me in that modern, French-made chopper, including the audio alarm on the portable EKG when it signaled that my heart was no longer beating. I noticed the modern glass panel, computer control display instead of the old analog gauges that I had known in my youth. My vision closed in and darkened, but I could still hear that EKG alarm clearly. A doctor later told me that hearing is one of the last senses to go.

My vision darkening on me was a curious phenomenon because of the way the darkness moved in from the sides so evenly like slowly closing the iris on a camera lens.

Then, as quickly as my heart momentarily stopped, it began beating again, and the oxygen mask that I was breathing from helped with the pain. Yet, curiously, I was not scared of dying. I was not denying my mortality, though. During the flight, I knew that these might be the last minutes of my existence.

I have seen the death of others too, so death is quite real to me. But in those past instances of violence, everything occurred so quickly that there was no time to be scared and most certainly no time for mental reflection. This was because I was in my combat frog brain modality.

But this time it was different. There was nothing I could do to help save my own life. All I could do was lie there, try to breath, and try and "think" to live. This time I did have those precious moments to think and reflect on my life.

The single thing that troubled me the most about dying was the tremendous impact it would have on my wife. But I transcended even this feeling as I knew that there was absolutely nothing I could do to spare her that experience. Death is simply a part of life too.

It was a crystalline moment for me. Perhaps my brain was starved of oxygen or there was some other medical reason for my odd mental state, but I think it was a genuine epiphany for me. I experienced a moment of great mental clarity. We are all hurling towards our death each moment. It is like we are born with an invisible digital clock over our heads that decrements to display how many years, months, days or seconds we have left in this world.

Yet, not one of us truly knows "what time it is." This is why we must actively and aggressively take charge of our lives and achieve personal freedom from fear.

I realized that when one is lying on their deathbed, the things they will regret the most are the things that *they did not do.* They regret much more the things they failed to try to accomplish than any of the things that they actually did.

Yet when I was close to death, I felt that I had done most of the things I had wanted and dreamed of doing as a young man. I had not let fear keep me from achieving them. I had suffered terribly for errors I had made in my youth, but I now simply saw those experiences as a part of who I was today. The dominant emotion I felt was that my life had truly been blessed.

Peace be with you all and:

"Think great thoughts, for you shall never be
Any greater than you think."